# THE MOTHER'S BOOK

## How to Survive the Molestation of Your Child

### Second Edition

## Carolyn M. Byerly, Ph.D.

**KENDALL/HUNT PUBLISHING COMPANY**
2460 Kerper Boulevard P.O. Box 539 Dubuque, Iowa 52004-0539

# Artistic Credits

**Photography:**  Carmen Mendoza, Radford, VA, and
Kathie Friesen, Seattle, WA.
**Typography and Layout:** Evelyn Roehl, Flying Fingers, Seattle, WA.
**Cover Design:** Teri Platt, Writing by Design, Tacoma, WA.

**ABOUT THE PHOTOGRAPHS: The women and children who appear** in the photos of this publication are models who volunteered in order to help illustrate the various ways that mothers have coped with and survived the molestation of their children. These models' personal lives do not necessarily represent the issues addressed in *The Mother's Book*.

# CONTENTS

# Acknowledgments

I am grateful to the many wise and courageous women who shared their stories and insights as mother survivors with me through the years toward the preparation of this current edition and the earlier (1985) edition of *The Mother's Book*. They remain the inspiration and purpose behind this project, and the book belongs to them.

Others deserving thanks include: Mariel Damaskin and the staff of Kendall/Hunt Publishing Company for supporting the book's publication these last six years; Pat Brown and the staff and volunteers of the Women's Resource Center, Radford, Virginia; the former clients, volunteers, and staff at Safeplace (women's shelter and rape crisis center) in Olympia, Washington; Evelyn Brom of the King County Prosecutor's Office, Seattle; Rev. Marie Fortune and the staff of the Center for the Prevention of Sexual and Domestic Violence, Seattle; Muriel Templeton, Richland, Washington; Trudy Hoy, Olympia, Washington; Florence Wolfe, Seattle; Kathleen Kennelly, formerly of the Sexual Assault Center, Seattle; the staff of King County Sexual Assault Resource Center, Renton, Washington; the Washington Coalition of Sexual Assault Programs; Rev. Joan Ham; and Kay McGraw.

I also want to express my gratitude to the many mother survivors who have called and written with comments after reading the earlier version of *The Mother's Book*. Your feedback, insight, and experiences shared unselfishly have often reminded me that *The Mother's Book* project is important to continue.

C.B.
Radford, VA, February 1992

Mothers often know <u>something</u> is wrong, but not <u>what</u> is wrong.
*Photo: C. Mendoza*

# Introduction

This second edition of *The Mother's Book* expands the original version, which was specifically concerned with mother's survival of their children's incest. The present edition tries to answer the call for information about mother's responses to both intra-familial and non-familial child sexual abuse.

In this way, the book tries to a fill a part of the knowledge gap that still surrounds women's personal experiences when their children are sexually abused. In the six years since *The Mother's Book* was first published, surprisingly little new information surfaced on the subject until Sandi Ashley's *The Missing Voice* (Kendall/Hunt, 1991) appeared. Ashley's book, a compilation of writings by mothers of incest victims, provides the first major resource of first-person statements and is an excellent complement to the present volume of *The Mother's Book*. We need similarly to hear from mothers whose children have been molested by non-family members.

This mother's survival guide grew out of a counseling session I had with a young mother in 1979, when I was working at a women's shelter and rape crisis center. "Ellen" sat beside me for two hours talking of her daughter's four-year molestation by a family member. Expressing her torment in learning about the incest, Ellen sorted through her options and began to make a plan for the next week. She was determined to survive her child's ordeal, thinking she could be more help to her daughter if she herself were strong. Her challenges were many, as her daughter's emotional problems were extensive and the family was having financial and health problems. She asked if there was something to read that would help her understand incest and the mother's experience.

At the time I could offer her only a pamphlet and list of two or three books, among them Sandra Butler's just published *Conspiracy of Silence: The Trauma of Incest* (New Glide, 1978). Nothing yet addressed mothers' own experience in incestuous families.

Ellen's keen sense of personal direction at a time of intense family crisis, like her request for printed information about mothers and incest, would be become familiar to those of us working in rape crisis centers. As the numbers of children disclosing sexual abuse rose in the early 1980s, rape crisis center staffs saw more and more mothers seeking support and information. Our staff members (many of us sexual assault survivors ourselves) grew better prepared to assist mother survivors as time went on because these women taught us the basic facts of their experience, their needs, and how to survive their children's molestation. Many mother survivors have, at some point, turned their own energies toward advocacy and support of victims and their mothers (through rape crisis programs and other channels).

My own most recent means of supporting mothers has been in helping to convey something of their experiences, insights, and successful skills for coping with their children's molestation.

The statements, stories, and most of the information contained in this book have come from mother survivors themselves, shared during individual and group interviews, through the loan of their journals and diaries, and in phone calls and letters. I have also drawn on my years of experience as an administrator and counselor/advocate at Safeplace women's shelter and rape crisis center in Olympia, Washington; on interviews and consultations with therapists, criminal justice, and child protective service personnel; and on current published research and clinical perspectives of those who work with victims and families affected by child sexual assault.

Through the years I have remained convinced that mothers are truly the forgotten parties in cases of incest and other child molestation. The attention of police, prosecutors, lawyers, and helping service personnel focuses mainly on the victim(s) and offender. Mothers too often are left to cope alone and to carry the extra burdens of solacing and caring for other family members in this stressful time. Few hands are extended to help her or to ask her how she feels and what she needs to get through the ordeal. The most unfortunate situations are those in which mothers are left not only with extensive caretaking of others, but are somehow held responsible for the child's victimization.

I have seen everyone from the victim to the prosecuting attorney ask mothers why they didn't do something to prevent the molestation. Any mother whose child has been molested feels emotionally distressed and will typically ask herself if there was any way she could have known about and prevented it. Any insinuation from others (especially those in authority positions) that she is in any way to blame for what the offender has done will deepen her emotional strife. Mothers caught in the tangled, dysfunctional web of incestuous family dynamics find particular pain in such insinuations. Usually troubled by a range of family problems, that may include her own abuse by the child's offender, she feels a profound helplessness and inability to cope when confronted with blame.

Except in those very rare cases where mothers themselves commit sexual abuse against their own or other children, mothers are not responsible for child molestation and incest, nor do they generally know the abuse is taking place. It is true that some children tell their mothers that someone has touched them and that the mothers don't believe or act to protect their children from further abuse. More common, however, is the mother who knows *something* is wrong with her child but not *what that something is*. The child may begin to behave in troubling ways, i.e., may be suddenly given to angry outbursts, to frequent masturbation (or other sexual behavior), to bedwetting (or other regressive behavior), with no apparent explanation. The mother may not suspect her child is being molested by her husband, older son, brother-in-law, Sunday school teacher, coach, babysitter, or neighbor, until the painful moment of disclosure.

"Julia" wasn't able to make sense of her adolescent son's behavior until she learned that her second husband had been molesting him for the past two years. She then agonized through the memories of son and husband eyeing each other across a room or spending long hours into the night together. The same trust and love for them that had allowed her to transcend suspicion of these events also, later, made the knowledge of incest almost unbearable. "Catherine" believed her disabled daughter had grown depressed because she was approaching adolescence and could not join in other children's social activities. She did not know that the child's physical therapist was sexually abusing the child twice a week until a school nurse told her. Catherine then suffered many painful recollections of seeing her daughter upset after physical therapy sessions and not understanding why.

If children are the primary victims of child sexual abuse, then mothers are the secondary victims. Mothers are faced with the pain of learning their children have been hurt, of helping and nurturing their children through the ordeal, and then having to struggle through their own uncertainties and trauma. There is no quick or easy way through these difficulties.

Most women do survive and go on in life, even though the experiences may leave scars for years to come. I have seen each woman I've known respond in her own unique way to very complex events, and, in the process, come into her own personal strength. The term mother *survivor* is an appropriate one for every woman who comes through the trauma of her child's molestation intact. In the years ahead, I hope more mother survivors will speak about their lives and the phenomenon of child sexual abuse.

# 1.

# Incest and Child Molestation

## INTRODUCTION

When sexual abuse became more visible in the early 1970s, it was as if a new "problem" had been discovered. In fact, the sexual violation of children is a cross-cultural phenomenon that has existed for a very long time. In the U.S., women's groups had begun speaking out against incest, molestation, and other forms of child abuse as early as the mid-nineteenth century. This early child welfare movement resulted in the first private child protective societies and, after the turn of the century, in a few state-sponsored child protective programs.

The remobilized women's movement of the 1960s brought child sexual abuse more forcefully into social consciousness. Large numbers of adult women speaking out publicly against their own experiences as sexually violated children drew renewed attention to the abuse many children still suffered. Rape crisis centers that began to open after 1972 offered 24-hour emotional support and assistance reporting.

By the mid 1970s, media coverage and the emergence of preventive education programs that encouraged children to tell someone if they were being sexually touched sparked renewed concern and action toward child protection and reforms in the legal and social services systems. Organized political lobbying on the part of women's organizations pushed through new legislation on rape and child sexual abuse between 1973 and the mid 1980s. *Chapter 4: Reporting Child Sexual Abuse,* explores the focus of new laws and the implications of reporting incest and child molestation.

The same social movement that sparked improved legislation also raised a number of fundamental questions: Why are children sexually abused? How widespread is the problem? What can we do to stop it?

## DEFINING CHILD SEXUAL ABUSE

Child sexual abuse is a general term that refers to a collection of erotic sexual activities between an adult and a child or even between children, usually of different ages. Those activities range from *non-physical sexual interactions*, such as voyeurism (watching a child undress or bathe, for instance), showing a child pornographic art or photos, talking in sexually explicit erotic language to a child, or exhibitionism (showing one's genitals to a child). Or the activities may involve *physical sexual interactions*, such as forcing or encouraging a child to engage in genital or breast touching, oral-genital acts, or vaginal, anal, or oral intercourse.

Even when the sexual activity occurs in a seemingly gentle, non-forced manner and children participate without resistance—as is often the case with incest—the activity is considered abusive. All such sexual activity betrays a child's innocence and trust, often by those on whom the child depends for care and nurturance. Sexual coercion or force also interrupts a child's normal sexual and emotional development and presents the child with feelings and experiences beyond their developmental ability to understand and handle responsibly.

The abuse is compounded when a child is made to keep the secret that sexual acts have occurred. The secrecy, often reinforced by threats of harm or by promises of special gifts or privileges, becomes an emotional burden that may seem overwhelming to the child.

## INCIDENCE OF CHILD SEXUAL ABUSE

Improved record keeping and expanded research since the mid 1970s have improved our information about the numbers of youth who may be sexually molested during their childhood or teen years. And yet we are far from an accurate assessment.

The numbers are least accurate in the documentation of incidence. In their book, *Sexual Abuse of Young Children* (Guilford Press, 1986), Kee MacFarlane and Jill Waterman discuss the problem of determining the extent of child victimization. They note that the figures from the American Humane Society's Clearinghouse on Child Abuse, which estimated 60,000 to 100,000 children in the late 1970s were sexually molested in the U.S. annually (affecting some 10-14% of American families) are suspect because only 31 states submitted data to the group in 1978.

Adding to the problem of incomplete data is the suspicion (on the part of the U.S. Department of Justice and other agencies) that most child molestation still goes unreported. This presumption is corroborated by studies among adult populations of women and men who say they never reported their victimization, and by interviews with convicted child molesters who disclose victimizing larger numbers of children than ever appear on police records.

Numbers become more accurate when incidence is estimated by research among the general public. Recent research by Diana E.H. Russell, reported in *Sexual Exploitation* (Sage, 1984), found that 16 percent of the 930 women in her study had been sexually abused by a family member and 31 percent had been molested by someone outside the family before age 18. In *Abused Boys* (Lexington Books, 1990), Mic Hunter uses current survey research to estimate that 50,000 to 90,000 boys under the age of 13 are molested each year in the U.S. Other research estimates that 10-20 percent of all child sexual abuse victims are male.

In nearly all cases of child sexual abuse (70-80%), the victim knows his/her offender. One-fourth to one-third of all child sexual abuse is believed to occur within families (i.e., is incestuous).

## PROFILE OF THE OFFENDER

Although incest and other child molesters may vary in personality, socioeconomic status, race, and personal interests, there are some characteristics that provide a common profile.

Persons who sexually abuse children are typically heterosexual adolescent and adult men who feel sexually and socially inadequate, particularly with peers. Offenders have usually experienced physical or sexual abuse themselves in childhood. Sexual gratification and a need to feel powerful motivate sexual offenders to cajole, trick, and force children to participate in sexual acts. Many select victims approximate the same age they were when someone abused them. They commit their acts against numerous young victims, mostly females, throughout their lives, unless stopped.

Sex offenders may lead lives that seem normal on the surface. They hold down jobs, participate in their communities, and may be prominent leaders in church, political, and other circles. They usually marry and have children. Those who are prone to abuse their own (or their wife's) children commonly become involved with a series of women who have young children.

Females occasionally molest their own or other children, but statistically female offenders are rare. Children abused by female offenders suffer the same trauma as those abused by men.

All child molesters have elaborate defense mechanisms that facilitate their behavior. Most deny their behavior and say that their young accusers are lying. Others admit that they had sex with the child(ren) accusing them, but they may justify it by saying that the child seduced them, that they were "teaching" the child about sex, or that there is nothing wrong with children having sex. This last argument is related to the efforts of groups of sex offenders to abolish child molestation laws in some states; their main argument is that children have a "right" to be sexual and to "consent" to sex at any age.

## SOCIAL FACTORS THAT ENABLE ABUSE

Child molesters are given tacit approval by society to use children for sexual gratification when nothing definitive is done to identify and stop them. There are a number of specific social factors that have enabled child molesters and incest offenders to victimize children.

Silence has been a powerful agent in the perpetuation of incest and other child molestation. The silence of victims has been reinforced by the stigma of sexual molestation, which has fallen primarily on the victims who have been allowed to feel ashamed and guilty for what has happened to them. Society has not, until recently, begun to direct responsibility more appropriately on offenders and to treat victims as the innocent parties.

Silence has also been encouraged by social tendencies to minimize the offender's behavior. Families and communities may have even joked about "dirty old men" without doing something to stop them from harming children. The "dirty old man" may be the uncle or grandfather who couldn't keep his hands off the children, the neighborhood joker who cornered the young girls for kisses, or the kindly old fool who insisted the kids sit on his lap and let him tickle them. The older females in families and neighborhoods, who may have been molested by the dirty old man as kids themselves, knew to keep their own children away from him, but speaking up and demanding he be reported to police and prosecuted has been a more recent development.

Child molestation also continues because of inadequate laws and a legal system that has traditionally favored adult rights over children's rights. Until strong child advocacy programs forced another approach, police and prosecutors were reluctant to take a child's word against an adult's. Because there are rarely witnesses to child sexual abuse, and children's testimony may seem less credible than an adult's, there has been a problem producing convincing legal evidence against offenders.

Incest and other offenses also continue because children are conditioned to obey adult authority. Unless a child has had prior adult encouragement to say "no" to others' demands for sex, or to "tell someone" if they are molested, he/she may be unprepared to protect themselves against sexual predators.

## ADDITIONAL FACTORS IN INCEST

Children are especially vulnerable in families where family members are allowed to keep secrets, where parents themselves come from abusive families of origin, and where authoritarian patterns dominate parent-child relationships. Incest offenders are masters of deceit and manipulation. They usually reign supreme over other family members, including their wives, and are unchallenged in their authority. They begin to "groom" their children (usually beginning with the eldest child first) early by establishing a special relationship or special times and places to be alone with the child. Grooming may feature bathing the child, showing the child nude photos (or explicit pornography), sexual talk, and progressively more intimate touching over a period of time until full genital contact occurs.

In order for incest offenders to continue their behavior, they elicit the trust of children and may threaten the child in some way. Telling the child that he (the offender) will go to jail, that mommy will leave, or that something terrible will happen to the family are common threats. Desperate or sadistic offenders may threaten to hurt or kill children who tell.

Although some offenders focus their abuse on only one child, most molest multiple victims. The victims may be unaware that other children are being molested in the family. In fact, some offenders gain a child's consent by promising to leave the sisters and brothers alone. Many offenders molest both girls and boys.

Child molesters rarely stop their behavior without legal intervention. There is, in fact, no way to make them accountable for their behavior without going through legal channels, which involves reporting to police, prosecutorial action (either trial or deferment), and long-term follow-up monitoring. Psychological evaluation during this process may determine that an offender is amenable for treatment for his offenses—an alternative to prison. Most offender treatment programs for child molesters, including incest offenders, now recognize that chances for repeat offenses are high, even after treatment. Child molesters are often compared to alcoholics, in terms of addictive behavior and the strong possibility for repeat violations.

# WORKING TO END CHILD SEXUAL ABUSE

The fact that most victims of incest of child molestation and incest are female and most offenders are male strongly suggests that this problem should be considered in a larger context. The secondary socio-economic and political position of females, vis-a-vis that of males, provides a starting point for analysis. For two decades now, women's groups have made a strong case for viewing child sexual victimization, rape, and wife battering as problems of sexual inequality. They advocate empowering female (and male) victims to speak publicly about their experiences and demand that social institutions (e.g., agencies, courts, lawmakers, and churches) assume responsibility for ending such violence against women, the usual victims. They advocate removing barriers to women's social equality in education, workplaces, public life, and family structures in order to stop female exploitation.

Incest and child molestation are unheard of in families and communities where parents share a mutual and equal position of authority, where feelings and thoughts are aired openly in an atmosphere of trust, where children are respected, and where there are no secrets. To bring about such an environment on a broader scale, society must change its values and institutional rules. The transformation will require the participation and work of many people for many years to come. We can all play a role in this process.

There is no single formula for getting through the emotional tangle after
your child discloses.
*Photo: C. Mendoza*

# 2.

# Disclosure

## INTRODUCTION

Mothers usually say that the moment they learned about their child's molestation remains both the most painful and memorable part of the ordeal. You may have learned about your child's molestation when the child told you herself (or himself), or when the child protective service worker arrived on your doorstep, or when the school principal called you. The following true stories, in which names are changed, provide three typical examples of how mothers learned and survived the disclosure of their children's abuse.

### Story #1: Sharon

Sharon's daughter Angie told her on a Friday afternoon. It was an angry disclosure following a disagreement between the two over how late that night Angie should stay out.

"What do you think we're going to do—have sex?" 16-year-old Angie asked her mother when Sharon questioned her about why she and her boyfriend couldn't be home by midnight. Before Sharon could answer, Angie added resentfully, "Well, it wouldn't be the first time anyway. It's no different than what dad has been doing to me—What are you going to do about *that*?"

### Story #2:  Ana

Ana learned about her daughter Maria's abuse from a caseworker from child protective services who had been called by school personnel. Seven-year-old Maria told her teacher and principal about her abuse after they had begun to put the pieces of the puzzle together on their own. They had watched Maria change over a period of weeks. Usually a cheerful little girl who liked school, Maria would grow quiet and withdrawn now on some mornings. She had taken to drawing her coat around her and refusing to take it off. Some days she would be the last on the bus, reluctant to go home. Her teacher had conferred with the principal about Maria's strange behavior, and together they had talked to Maria. Maria said that her stepfather made her do things that scared her. The teacher and principal called child protective services, and that same afternoon a caseworker came to talk with Maria.

### Story #3:  Melanie

Melanie found out that her son Justin had been molested by his babysitter one summer afternoon. Melanie thought it was odd that Justin, 4, had been rubbing his bottom. "Do you have an itch?" she had asked him. "No, it hurts," Justin had answered. She asked if she could see what was wrong, and Justin gave a strong, "No!" Thinking her child might have a rash that needed treating, Melanie eventually inspected the child's anus and found excessive redness and bruising. Justin finally and reluctantly explained that the 14-year-old boy down the block, who had stayed with Justin a week before, had taken Justin up to play in the treehouse. There he had tried to engage in anal intercourse with Justin. The babysitter had made Justin promise not to tell, adding that "Nobody will believe you anyway." Melanie assured Justin that she believed him and that this wouldn't happen again to him.

## MOTHERS' FEELINGS

Mothers report a wide range of emotional responses to their children's disclosures of abuse. Responses vary according to the number of other crises present in a mother's life, her experience handling crises, whether or not she was a victim of abuse herself, the nature of her relationship with the child, her level of self-esteem and self-confidence, her knowledge of sexual abuse and where to go to for help, religious and cultural teachings about sexuality and abuse, her values and belief system, etc.

Sharon described her initial reaction to Angie's disclosure as one of numbness and distance. She said:

> *I felt like I was in the middle of a slow-motion movie. I wondered if I was watching this happen to someone else. What Angie was telling me seemed incredible. Was she lying, I asked myself. I knew I should stay calm and figure this out. Since I couldn't feel anything anyway, that wasn't really a problem. I thought I should do something, but I wasn't sure what. I kept thinking back, and the last few years passed before me. . . All the clues were there, but I hadn't understood them. I knew Angie had to be telling the truth. Angie and I were able to talk after a while, and we made a plan for what we were going to do.*

Ana registered anger and fear when the CPS caseworker told her about her daughter's sexual abuse by Ana's new husband:

> *I was so mad at him! How could he do this to Maria? And, then I was mad at Maria—why didn't she tell me? I would have stopped it! Then I sat down and thought about what this really meant, and I just felt scared. In a few hours he could be in jail. And even if they didn't arrest him, I could never bring myself to be with him again. The children and I could starve. I didn't make enough money for us to live on. What were we going to do?*

Melanie felt incredibly guilty and sad when she learned about Justin's abuse:

> *I felt like crying, but I wanted to seem strong and together for Justin. I wanted to comfort him, to make this go away, to*

*make him feel okay again. When I saw the damage the boy had done to my son, I felt a deep loss for him. His innocence was gone. Why had I left Justin with this kid—I hardly even knew him. Somehow I felt responsible. Later, after talking to the rape crisis advocate, I realized that I still felt the grief and sadness over my own sexual abuse. When I was six, an older cousin had raped me on a family picnic. He told me he'd kill me if I ever told anyone. And so I never had. The cousin raped me two more times before his parents moved to another city. My childhood seemed to end after I was abused. Would Justin's childhood be over too, I wondered?*

These stories illustrate some of the most common reactions that mothers have when learning their children have been molested. These and other reactions may be summarized as follows.

**Numbness.** Inability to experience any emotion or physical sensation. Some women describe this as "being in shock." This is a stage of trauma that may last from only a few minutes to several hours.

**Distance.** A feeling of being separated from people and events around you. This reaction may be your way of stepping back and looking at what is happening. It buys you time before the reality floods in on you and demands that you respond.

**Anger.** Many mothers feel angry at everyone around them, a kind of general anger. Others experience anger at someone in particular—the child for "doing this," the offender for violating the child and/or betraying you, yourself for not doing a good job of protecting your child. You may also be angry at the CPS worker who brought this to light (or took your child away), or at others in the legal and helping service systems. Anger can be a powerful and useful emotion if directed at the offender who made all this happen.

**Disbelief.** You may keep asking yourself if this is real, how this could be possible, if you are dreaming. Disbelief usually gives way to other feelings as you accumulate information and come to grips with the child's experience.

**Denial.** You may not believe your child, especially if the offender continues to deny the accusations and you have little or no evidence of the child's truthfulness. You may even resist accepting evidence when it exists. Denial is a way we protect ourselves from emotional pain. Since children rarely lie about sexual abuse, you will want to explore the information at hand and accept its veracity. You cannot really be supportive to the child(ren) involved until you have moved through the denial stage.

**Shame.** The feeling of shame is especially common in incestuously abusive families. You may feel that you have participated in what has happened somehow. Or you may feel dirty and ashamed for having had sex with the same man who abused your child(ren). You may fear what others will think of you and your family when they find out. Your own self-worth may seem lowered by the abuse. If shame is a strong response in you, you may want to examine the different ways it entered into your life before the disclosure. This is a powerful, important emotion to explore with a counselor.

**Invisibility.** Mothers say they sometimes feel insignificant and invisible after their children are sexually abused. All the attention is suddenly focused on the child victim(s), the offender, and any other children in the family. Your feelings and needs may seem secondary to everyone else's, especially if you believe your role as a mother is to help and nurture others and that you are supposed to put your own needs aside. While this may seem a natural predicament for a mother to be in, you will want to stop and take stock of your own needs at this time. You do matter and your survival is critical to your own future and your child's.

**Guilt and self-blame.** Feelings that this is all your fault may overcome you. You may blame yourself for not protecting your child, for not having suspected what went on, and for all sorts of other things. Mothers develop an uncanny ability to take on responsibility that isn't theirs. If this becomes your problem, remember, you did not commit the molestation—the offender did. You are not the guilty party in this situation.

**Hurt and betrayal.** In the case of incestuous abuse, you may feel hurt and betrayed by your husband (or partner, or another relative), as well as by your child. Feelings of betrayal are particularly common when fathers/ stepfathers have engaged in sexual relations with adolescent daughters, making you feel like the outsider. The hurt is especially profound because they have worked so hard to keep it secret, even to scheme against you. They have taken your love and trust for granted, and operated in the home environment that you considered safe and sacred.

**Jealousy.** In the case of incest, it is not unusual for mothers to feel jealous of the sexual relationship that their daughters (and even sons) have shared with their husbands or partners. The child has assumed the place of intimacy that you thought was yours, has seemingly become "the other woman." One mother, whose daughter was molested from age 7-14 by her second husband, said that each time she felt jealous, she would take out the photo of her daughter at the age of the abuse to remind herself that it was this small, vulnerable child who fell prey to her husband's assaults. Each time, her jealousy faded into anger.

**Sexual inadequacy or rejection.** Incestuous abuse often makes mothers question their own sexual attractiveness and adequacy, as well as experience feelings of rejection by the offender who preferred the child. If you have this fear, remind yourself that it is a psychologically disturbed man who seeks out a child for sexual gratification. Your sexual qualities were not a factor in his irresponsible, unhealthy behavior.

**Religious concerns.** You may ask yourself if God has punished you by allowing your child to be abused. Or you may wonder if God is testing your husband or partner (particularly in the case of incest). You may also feel that your options for coping with this situation are limited by your religious beliefs, particularly if you have not heard this problem discussed by your clergy or church members. It is important for you to talk over your concerns with a member of the clergy who has been trained in sexual abuse issues and who is supportive to you and your child(ren). It is essential that you receive affirmation, not condemnation, at this time. (Note that *Chapter 7: Common Religious Issues*, provides a fuller discussion of this topic.)

**Minimizing the seriousness.** You may tell yourself that what has happened is not very serious, that your child won't really be affected by this, that the offender really didn't mean to harm anyone, and that you can forgive and forget. This is a time for a reality check: Sexual abuse *is* very serious, even if it only happens once. There is almost a certain chance that it *will* have short- and long-term effects on your child and others involved.

**Revenge.** You may want to get even with your child's offender. You may even find yourself plotting ways of getting revenge. This is a common response but one that must be thought through carefully. Consider productive ways of getting even, ones that you can live with later on and that will benefit you and your child. Consider some alternatives—confronting the offender, using the legal system, publicizing the offender's identity, suing him, etc.

**Financial and other fears.** Incestuous abuse, when the family breadwinner is the offender, generates worries in many mothers of what will happen to the family. If you separate from or divorce your husband, or if he loses his job over the allegations of incest, there may be financial changes ahead for your family. This is a serious and concrete issue for many families, and one which must be addressed. Most women find this issue easier to think about once the crisis stage is past and they can consider their economic alternatives.

**A desire to protect him.** This response, especially acute in women whose husbands are remorseful for what they have done, can be particularly debilitating. One consequence could be competing feelings of loyalty to your child and husband. Your protective, maternal feelings for him should be examined closely, as they may be masking unidentified symptoms of dysfunction in your relationship with the offender. Adult, mature relationships do not require spouses to protect each other from responsibility for serious acts.

**Hatred.** This feeling is an extension of anger and may accompany your need to distance yourself from the child's offender. Your hatred for him may be directed both at his behavior and the trauma and chaos that his behavior has caused. Hatred sometimes strengthens resolution to see the situation through in all of its complicated requirements.

**Repulsion.** Women often report feeling repulsed physically by husbands and partners who molest their children. Some women even experience nausea when the offender approaches them sexually. This is a normal response and can serve to remind you that you have every right to keep your distance from this person who has betrayed you and brought pain to your family.

**Confusion and doubt.** You may be uncertain of what to do from one moment to the next, unsure of whom to trust (and confide in), how to comfort your child, etc., both during the initial crisis and later on.

You may find yourself doubting your coping skills, your judgment, and your ability to make sound decisions for yourself and your children. These feelings may seem to stymie you and lock you in a kind of limbo.

## COPING WITH THE FEELINGS

It is important for you to explore these initial feelings, as well as those that will arise later on. There is no single formula for getting through the emotional tangle during and after the initial disclosure of your child's sexual abuse. However, nearly every mother suggests finding immediate support —someone to talk to who will believe you, who can provide emotional reassurance, and who is willing to be an intelligent sounding board for you.

Some moms have such supporters in their extended families or social networks. Others prefer the support and assistance of rape crisis counselors, available through local sexual assault centers and women's shelters on a 24-hour crisis basis. Rape crisis counselors are trained to listen to you, help you sort out feelings, accompany you and your child to agencies and court, and make referrals to longer-term counseling. (Note, a partial list of such services appears in a state-by-state listing in the Directory at the end of this book.)

## FIRST STEPS AFTER DISCLOSURE

In addition to locating support, here are several basic first steps to follow after you learn your child has been sexually molested:

**Believe the child.** Young children almost never lie about having been sexually touched or otherwise violated. While teens are statistically slightly more likely to fabricate a story of abuse, they too rarely disclose a violation that has not occurred. Accepting your child's story will help you to cope with your own emotional reactions to the abuse and to make the many decisions about your own and your family's future now before you.

**Talk with your child.** Tell the child that what has happened is not her/his fault and that you are going to protect her/him from further abuse. Assure the child that she/he can trust you with the information about the abuse. Reassure the child that it was good that she/he told someone about the abuse. Begin to rebuild any bonds you feel have been damaged by the abuse.

**Report the abuse to police or child protective services.** This is a perhaps threatening but important step to take. What happened to your child can only be stopped with legal intervention. Even counseling for the offender requires a legal mandate and long-term monitoring. (Note, *Chapter 4: Reporting Child Sexual Abuse*, provides details on this step.)

**Confronting the offender.** This is an optional step that you may want to consider, particularly if the offender is your husband or someone else close to your family. Confrontation is usually more successful when planned and thought out. Consider what you need to say to the offender and what, if any, questions you want to put to him. Develop responses to his denials and rationalizations.

**Trust yourself.** You have many years as a woman and mother behind you, and you have learned a great deal of useful knowledge through these life experiences. Trust yourself to get through this crisis. However, you need not do this on your own. You have the right to ask for support through this devastating time. And you can pull through as so many others have done.

Most mothers say they needed someone to talk to, to believe them and listen to their feelings.
*Photo: C. Mendoza*

3.

# Mothers' Needs After Disclosure

## INTRODUCTION

Mothers' reactions to their children's molestation will be followed by a complex set of needs, some emotional and others more concrete. Following are some of the most often mentioned needs experienced by mothers after disclosure.

## NEEDS AFTER DISCLOSURE

**"Someone to talk to."** Most mothers say they needed "someone to believe me" and "someone I could trust" to tell what happened to their child. This person—or persons—might be a friend, a member of the family (mothers and sisters are high on the list), a minister with knowledge of child molestation and incest, or a rape crisis advocate. Mothers are also hoping to hear this trusted person(s) say, "This wasn't your fault," when they talk about the child's molestation and their feelings. Your need for one or more confidantes may continue for some time—weeks or months after the disclosure.

**"Someone to counsel me about my own molestation/incest."** There is nothing like your child's disclosure to bring back all the feelings and memories of your own abuse. If you haven't talked to anyone about your childhood molestation, or if you are experiencing retraumatization even after you thought you'd worked this all out, now is an important time to address this problem. You may not only find it helpful but essential to you in order to face the realities of your child's abuse. A rape crisis advocate or a private therapist with training in sexual assault can be a good support to you in this.

**"To know what happened."** Most mothers say that it is painful but important for them to know the truth of the molestation—the nature, extent and frequency of the abuse, the time and place(s), the child feelings.

**"To know I wasn't the first mother this happened to."** This is usually best achieved by meeting and talking to other mothers who have survived incest and child molestation in their families. Ask your rape crisis center or child protective service worker about mothers' groups.

**"To have a break from him."** In families where incest has occurred, mothers express the need for a physical separation from the offender in order to gain perspective, consider their feelings about the relationship, and "to break the game we were caught up in," as one mother put it. Most women find it essential that the offender leave home, either temporarily or permanently.

**"To be treated as a person."** You will want to have your feelings listened to seriously, to feel respected, to be acknowledged when you are present, to be cared about and not taken for granted by children, friends, or people in the "system."

**"To regain control of my own life and mind."** Particularly in cases of incest, mothers express the need to recover a sense of control over day-to-day events and their personal thoughts. As a woman and mother caught in the dynamics of an incestuous family, you may have lost a feeling of ownership for these things over a period of time, even without realizing it. You can feel more in charge of yourself and your life again, particularly with the support of friends and counselors.

**"To obtain basic information on survival."** Day-to-life can become overwhelming when your child has been sexually abused. You may need new kinds of information—about police, courts, treatment (for child, yourself, your family), prevention of further abuse, stress reduction in your life, etc. Rape crisis centers are a good source of basic information and referral to other services.

**"To understand how my husband's battering (of me) was related to the incest."** Many men who incestuously abuse their children also physically abuse their wives. If you are a victim of battering, you will have a separate set of issues to address in counseling—beyond those related specifically to your child's sexual abuse.

**"To make basic life decisions."** Should you move to a new neighborhood or city to avoid public attention? In the case of incest, leave or divorce your husband? Tell relatives, friends, school teachers, neighbors about your child's abuse? You will have many questions facing you. These are some of them, but new, unanticipated questions may arise in the course of events. Mothers advise taking time to answer questions that aren't urgent. For the urgent ones, seek the advice of those you trust or a rape crisis advocate.

**"To know my options regarding custody."** In the case of incest, your child may have been placed in the protective custody of a foster family. You should know your rights and options regarding custody and the ins and outs of the legal system. "Don't sign anything without knowing your rights," advises one mother who, under stress, signed away custody of her daughter to another relative following incest disclosure. You will want to investigate these matters and take as much time as necessary before making decisions. *Chapter 4: Reporting Child Sexual Abuse* provides some information to help inform you. Rape crisis advocates in your area will be more familiar with your state's laws and procedures.

**"To know how my daughter/son and the other children will react."** Like other mothers, you may worry about signs of trauma in your child who was victimized, as well as her/his siblings. Everyone in the family is affected by child molestation, particularly when the abuse has been within the family. There are several ways you can educate yourself about the signs of trauma and other problems. Read up on the subject—*Recommended Reading* at the end of this book contains some suggestions. Talk with a rape crisis advocate about effects of molestation on children and other family members. Ask other mothers who have survived this situation for their insights. (See *Chapter 5: Parenting Issues*.)

**"To make sure this won't happen again."** Taking steps to safeguard your child from continued sexual abuse is important. In the case of incest, this usually entails understanding legal ground rules (such as how and when the court will permit contact between child and offender) and guidelines for interaction laid down by the offender's court-appointed therapist. The therapist's guidelines will probably involve an agreement that the offender will not be alone with the child until she/he is 21, and that the contact will not be sexual in any way. All mothers can help protect their children from future victimization by teaching them assertiveness, and by encouraging children to tell you or another adult if someone tries to engage them sexually. Children over the age of 6 can also benefit from taking a self-defense course or training in martial arts. Self-protection is a life-long process that should begin at this time.

## FACING THE MEMORIES

Once your child has told you about the molestation, you can expect what one mother described as a "flood of memories" to come over you. You may continue to be haunted by your child's story and trauma for some months to come. You will continue to examine your own relationship to the abuse and wonder what you could have done to prevent this, to know that it was happening, and to have stopped it sooner. (Note: While these are natural reflections, they should be put in context through counseling or other supportive interactions so that you can stop feeling responsible for what the offender has done.)

Incestuous abuse makes the memories especially pervasive. As you piece together the events, and the bigger picture (and your location in it) comes into focus, you should prepare yourself to contend with moments of painful insight. At the least expected moment—when you're in a crowd, driving your car, walking through the rooms of your house—new realizations will come to you and dominate your thoughts. Each new memory can bring with it both old and new emotions, and possibly tears of rage and anguish. You can anticipate the issue of memories and put your support network "on call." Tell your special support people they may hear from you at odd times of the day and night. Remind yourself that while remembering can be painful, it also enables you to come to terms with the whole truth of your child's molestation and deal more realistically with what has happened.

## RELATIONSHIP WITH THE OFFENDER

Making decisions about how and whether to maintain interaction with a child molester known to your family raises some complicated questions. All sorts of things will enter into the solutions you define for yourself.

**Proximity** to the offender (if he is a neighbor or someone else you or your child may run into) can make you feel trapped, threatened and resentful. If he is a member of your immediate or extended family, you may feel his presence close in around you. You can define the physical distance between the offender and you and your children necessary to make you feel safe and out of his sphere. Also consider the means you have to enforce this distance—the legal system? The help of friends or family? Your own assertive boundary setting?

**Emotional attachment** is one of the most powerful factors affecting mothers' future relationship to their children's molesters. In the case of a husband or partner, common issues include whether or not you love him, whether or not you feel you can ever trust him again, religious or cultural beliefs about divorce, economic factors (namely, can you survive without him), his willingness to undergo counseling and change, and his feelings toward you and your child(ren). If the molester is another of your children (e.g., the victim's brother), you may feel torn by competing parental urges to nurture and to punish. When the molester is a member of the extended family or friendship circle, you are confronted by how to renegotiate complex patterns of interaction.

Most mothers need time and personal counseling to make short- and long-term decisions about divorce, custody, and to redefine their relationships to offenders who are relatives or family acquaintances. However, some mothers know immediately after disclosure what they want to do. In both cases, some period of no contact can be helpful while you gain perspective on what has happened, begin to rebuild (or strengthen) bonds with your child, and look at your options.

Women whose husbands or partners were the offenders, and who decide to remain in a relationship with the men, face deeply personal questions around re-establishing trust, sexual contact, openness, and a relationship based on equality (in terms of respect, shared responsibilities and privileges).

**Re-establishing sexual relationships with incest offenders** presents many women with particular concern. "It was hard for me to get over feeling repulsed by him," one woman said, adding that even though she loved and wanted to stay with him, that it was nearly a year before she could stand to have him touch her. Couple counseling is essential if the relationship is to continue. This is usually offered as part of the treatment package for offenders who remain with their partners. Establishing new grounds for respect and rebuilding sexual bonds as well as new patterns of non-sexual affection are important. Sex should be mutually pleasurable and loving. You have a right to have your sexual likes and needs satisfied in this relationship.

## STANDING UP FOR YOURSELF

Your feeling of self-worth and your ability to stand up for yourself and be assertive will greatly enhance your survival as a woman and mother. Standing up for yourself may be hard if this has not been part of your experience. You may be faced with learning some new skills—how to express feelings and thoughts, how to feel and show anger, how to convey your wishes and expectations of others, and how to reject unwarranted criticism.

It may be helpful for you to spend a number of personal counseling sessions examining your own feelings about yourself in order to begin learning these skills. Assertiveness is a way of life and one you can learn as you go. To gain some basic skills, you may want to take a course in assertiveness techniques or read a book on the subject. If you locate a mothers' support group, you can practice with other group members.

One major goal of learning assertiveness is to avoid being influenced or controlled by those close to you, particularly those with whom you are sexually involved. This will help you maintain your own identity and avoid getting caught in abusive dynamics in the future.

## IF YOU ARE A BATTERED WOMAN

Most families where incest occurs also experience other symptoms of dysfunction. One problem often present is domestic violence —emotional, physical, and sexual abuse of one or more family members by another family member. Incest is one form of domestic violence. So is spouse abuse, or "battering."

You are technically a "battered woman" if you experience any of the following:

**Emotional abuse,** i.e., he calls you names (like ugly, slut, bitch), puts you down, tells you no one else will want you (if you leave him), treats you like a child, isolates you from friends and family members, withholds affection, ignores you, threatens you or the children with harm, threatens he'll commit suicide unless you do certain things.

**Physical abuse,** i.e., he keeps you at home, holds you down (or otherwise restrains you), pushes or shoves you, slaps you (open-handed), punches you (fist), hits you with objects, throws things at you, kicks you, uses (or threatens to use) guns, knives or other weapons to control you.

**Sexual acts,** i.e., he calls you sexual names, makes jokes about your body, criticizes you as a lover, forces you to make love when you don't want to, holds you and forces sex on you, makes you do things you don't like, tortures you physically during sex, engages in affairs with other women (either secretly or blatantly), compares your love-making to other women's.

It is important for you to acknowledge these experiences and to address their effect on your life. Most women's shelters offer a safe haven to get you and your children to safety, if this is necessary. Shelters also sponsor support groups for abused women. Most states now protect wives and partners from domestic abuse—you can ask the shelter about laws and services in your area.

## IF YOUR VICTIM CHILD IS MALE

As discussed in *Chapter 1*, current research now indicates that the number of male victims is much higher than once thought—some researchers believe as many as a fourth to a half of those molested. Researchers believe that male victimization is not reported for several reasons. First, there is a homophobic stigma surrounding male victimization by male offenders. Victims, parents, and those in legal and social systems may believe that homosexual contact in general is shameful and wrong. They may suspect that there is something psychologically abnormal about *both* offender and victim. If such values and attitudes are operating, you may find that adults in charge are not distinguishing between sexual relations between consenting males in general and the particular instance of sexual abuse of your child by a male offender.

Second, social norms around masculinity create a context in which it is still difficult to address male victimization. Expectations that males should be strong and care for themselves (even as children and teens) make it difficult for boys to tell someone they've been violated. Everyone from the victim to those they tell may believe he should have been able to prevent the abuse. In addition, there is a general belief that sexual abuse is less harmful to males than to females because boys are "tougher" in dealing with difficulties. These are myths, of course. Boys experience pain and trauma from sexual molestation, just as girls do, and they need to be able to talk about it and to have adults protect them.

Third, social definitions of male and female roles may confuse the issue of young male victimization by female offenders. While statistically rare, such abuse exists and may be significantly underreported. Young males molested by mothers or caretakers may not interpret sexual touch as inappropriate because they are used to being touched and held intimately by females throughout their infancy and childhoods. Adolescent males molested by an older female outside the family may interpret their experience as a first sexual encounter. One man in his thirties said he thought he was just getting his first "lay" when the middle-aged woman in the next apartment building had intercourse with him just before his thirteenth birthday. He had bragged to the other boys about it but told no adults.

More publicity around the definition of incest and sexual molestation in recent years has allowed many men and boys to gain new understanding of early life sexual experiences and to begin speaking out. Mic Hunter's book, *Abused Boys: The Neglected Victims of Sexual Abuse* (Lexington Books, 1990) provides a needed resource on this topic.

Male victims experience most of the traumatic problems that females do. Some also have concerns about their sexuality—confusion about whether having been molested by a man means he (the victim) is homosexual. Rage and angry acting-out are common in male victims who feel they failed in stopping the abuse or feel helpless, guilty, dirty or unworthy because of what has happened to them.

Mothers nearly always find it helpful to have their sons talk with a counselor who is trained to work with male victims and who is comfortable around issues of sexual identity and knowledgeable about pedophilia. It contributes to the male child's healing when the sexual abuse is treated seriously by those who interact with the child. Mothers and legal advocates at rape crisis centers can put necessary pressure on police, prosecutors, and others in the system to respond the same to male victimization as they would to female abuse.

## IF YOU ARE A LESBIAN MOTHER

Lesbian mothers say their sexual orientation often becomes an issue when incest is disclosed. Sometime the issues arise early after the disclosure, particularly in contact with child protective services or other legal systems whose representatives may be take your lifestyle into consideration when making decisions about your suitability for parenting your child(ren).

Your sexual orientation may arise again in court when the offender goes to trial, or when long-term custody is being decided. Or it may surface in the context of the crisis created by the molestation, when your child discloses a wider array of concerns in her/his life, some of them surrounding your personal life.

If your sexual orientation has become an issue in your child's case for any reason, you may want to take some extra steps. One is to seek joint counseling for you and your child with a supportive therapist who has training in sexual identity as well as child molestation. A second is to consult an attorney on custody matters—an attorney familiar with the legal issues of lesbian mothers as well as child molestation.

## TAKING TIME FOR YOURSELF

Finding time and feeling that you have a *right to take time for yourself* becomes many mothers' greatest long-term problem. There are a million excuses why mothers don't take more time for themselves—nearly all of them real and logical. But your own time and space are important. At first it may be only a few minutes during the day to think, read, visit a friend, or go someplace away from the atmosphere of crisis. Plan to take time for yourself *regularly*.

This is part of gaining (or regaining) a sense of your own identity, a time to plan and dream. Children can and do learn to respect mother's time to herself, if you define it and stick to it. Here's a plan that may work for you:

**Step 1**     Schedule your time (exact time, date and place) on your calendar.

**Step 2**     Decide what you'll do.

**Step 3**     Tell anyone who needs to know that you will be gone (or unavailable) for the time you've set. Explain that this is your personal time. You'll be back later.

**Step 4**     Take care of details—finding child care, arranging transportation, etc.

**Step 5**     Enjoy yourself!

**Suggested activities:** Take a walk, go to the library, see a film, go to lunch or have a picnic with a friend, go out to dinner, read, sew, jog (or do something else active), join an exercise class, take a class on a subject you've wanted to know more about, write in your journal, garden, drive to a place you haven't been before, go away for the day or the weekend.

## KEEPING A RECORD

You may find it helpful to keep some form of personal record of these weeks and months when you are as vitally concerned with your own survival as you are your child's. Begin with the experience of disclosure—what happened, how you felt, how you coped. Make entries often enough to provide a record for yourself to look back on later. You can chart changes in your knowledge of the situation, perceptions, attitudes; note the new people you meet; note the events and feelings in daily life.

## FINDING SUPPORT

The number one key to surviving your child's molestation will be finding and maintaining a "support system." This is the unanimous recommendation of mothers who have been through the experience. Your support system may be as small as one or two people, or as large as dozens. The important thing is to know you have people in your life with whom you can talk about the incest or molestation, as well as the other issues you're struggling to address. You need to know that someone else cares about you during this time.

Support is sometimes available through family members, churches, friendships you already have. If you feel safe and comfortable telling one or more people you already know about the incest or molesta-tion, you will have a relatively easy time developing your support net-work. If you are reluctant or anguished talking about what has happened, or you believe that your family and friends will not understand, then you may want to use a different strategy to find the support you need.

The rape crisis center in your community is one place you can turn. The professional and volunteer staff will be trained to talk to you about your situation and experienced in helping you report, work with legal and other systems, and locate longer-term counseling. A rape crisis counselor can help you sort out your feelings, identify options for decisions, and so forth. Most centers have a 24-hour crisis line to be available to you around the clock. Some centers also sponsor mother's support groups to let mothers like yourself share feelings and help each other through the aftermath of child molestation.

If you want to talk to someone from your own particular ethnic or religious group, feel free to ask the rape crisis center personnel if such a person is available. Most rape crisis centers today make an effort to serve a diverse clientele and try to be sensitive to individual needs by better training their own staffs and by actively networking with a broad range of community groups. (Also see *Chapter 8: Issues in Mothers' Recovery*.)

Mothers usually find the experience of reporting and going through the system easier with an advocate.
*Photo: K. Friesen*

## 4.

# Reporting Child Sexual Abuse *

## INTRODUCTION

The general public became concerned about the many forms of child abuse during the 1960s, when social movements brought them to public attention. Since then, all 50 states, Guam, Puerto Rico, and the Virgin Islands have passed some form of legislation to protect children. Sexual abuse is covered under these statutes.

Most of these laws require persons working in certain occupations to report suspected sexual and other forms of child abuse. Physicians, nurses (and other health care workers), therapists, social service personnel, and child care workers are included among these. Laws also allow any other concerned person who suspects child abuse or neglect to report it and to remain anonymous.

You may report the suspected molestation of your child, whether the offender is a relative or a nonfamily member. Reports should be made to local law enforcement or to another agency responsible for handling child abuse cases (for example, a child protective services office or state department of social service).

This section reviews general issues related to reporting child sexual abuse, as well as some particular legal considerations. The laws of Washington state provide the reference for most of the discussion.

* The author would like to thank Evelyn K. Brom, Special Assault Unit, King County Prosecuting Attorney's Office, Seattle, for her assistance in revising this chapter.

Washington state laws and services related to child sexual molestation have been a model for other states. However, your child's abuse will be covered under the laws of the state(s) in which the abuse occurred.

## PROBLEMS THAT SHOULD BE REPORTED

While the definition of child abuse may vary slightly from state to state, most laws include neglect, physical injury, emotional harm, and sexual abuse and exploitation. Increasingly, states also are passing laws making it illegal to possess, produce, or distribute child pornography.

## SEXUAL OFFENSES DEFINED BY LAW

The Revised Code of Washington divides laws defining sexual offenses against children into the following categories: (1) first, second, and third degrees of rape of a child, (2) first, second, and third degrees of molestation of a child, (3) first and second degrees of incest, (4) first and second degrees of sexual misconduct with a minor, and (5) communicating with a minor for immoral purposes. Familial child molestation (incest) may be prosecuted under any of these laws.

Rape charges against persons 16 years of age or older require that there was forced or coerced sexual intercourse of the victim by the perpetrator. "Sexual intercourse" is defined as the penetration however slight of the vagina or anus by a sex organ or other object, or sexual contact involving the sex organs of one person and the mouth of the other, whether those persons were of the same or opposite sex. The degree of the crime generally depends on the ages of victim and perpetrator.

"Sexual contact," which figures centrally in molestation charges, also includes touching of the sexual or other intimate parts of a person for the purpose of gratifying the sexual desire of either party.

Washington state's sexual assault laws consider factors like "mental capacity" and "physical helplessness." Mental capacity concerns the victim's condition at the time of the offense which prevented her or him from understanding the nature or consequences of the act of sexual intercourse, whether that condition was produced by illness, defect, the influence of a substance, or some other cause. Physical helplessness means a person was unconscious or for some other reason physically unable to communicate unwillingness to engage in a sexual act.

Washington state also has "sexual predator" laws that require both juveniles and adults convicted of a sexual offense to register with the sheriff in the county where they reside. Failure to register is a crime.

In Washington state, incest and child rape may be reported up to five years after the last incident of abuse. Other forms of child sexual abuse may be reported up to seven years from the last incident.

## LEGAL ADVOCACY AND ASSISTANCE FOR MOTHERS

It is easy to become frustrated and confused by all of the people who suddenly get involved with your and your child's lives after incest or molestation is disclosed. Child protective service workers, police officers, prosecutors and lawyers, judges, and therapists may be some of these people.

Mothers usually find the experiences of reporting and going through the legal system easier when they have a legal advocate who is trained to help them interpret the legal proceedings. Legal advocates can explain the steps involved in reporting, the role of prosecutors and other officials, your parental rights, and court proceedings. Legal advocates can also lend emotional support when legal proceedings become drawn out over many weeks or months. In Washington state (and most other states) you have the right by law to have an advocate of your choice with you during legal proceedings (interviews, court hearings, trials).

You can locate an advocate through your local rape crisis center or women's shelter. Some prosecutors offices also provide advocacy to mothers through victim assistance programs.

## CHILD PROTECTIVE SERVICES (CPS)

In Washington state, Child Protective Service (CPS) agencies are responsible for assuring that incest (sexual abuse within the family) allegations are investigated and that the children involved are protected from further abuse. CPS is a state agency, part of the Department of

Social and Health Services. CPS offices are located in local communities throughout the state.

Although CPS is responsible for seeing that cases are investigated and referred to law enforcement, CPS workers do not have the legal authority either to conduct official police investigations or to remove children from homes. However, the role of CPS workers becomes closely intertwined in these activities. Police and sheriff's officers call upon CPS workers to include their professional assessments in police reports and to offer their recommendations regarding the need to remove the offender or child from homes where the child's safety is in question.

In addition, prosecutors often require CPS workers to testify in court regarding their initial findings in the evaluation of incest reports and, under some circumstances, what the child (under 10) told them about the abuse. As a representative (and employee) of the state, CPS workers take on official responsibilities that prevent them from serving as an independent advocate for you.

## SEQUENCE OF EVENTS IN INCEST CASES

The following is a usual sequence of legal events in Washington state when suspected incest is reported to Child Protective Services.

(1) **The report (made by you or a third party) is assigned to a CPS caseworker.** The initial information is recorded and forwarded to a CPS caseworker for follow-up.

(2) **Caseworker makes an initial assessment.** On the basis of details provided in the initial report, the caseworker will talk with your child at school or another neutral location. The purpose of this initial screening is to gather sufficient information to determine if there is a likelihood that abuse has occurred. The caseworker uses established risk assessment protocol in this screening.

(3) **Caseworker makes recommendations regarding safety of child and the need for police investigation.** If the caseworker believes your child has been molested by someone in your family household, she or he will usually request that the offender leave home until the case has been investigated and the court decision rendered. If the suspected offender is unwilling to leave, the caseworker may ask

police to intervene. In some cases, CPS may obtain a protective order to assist in protecting the child.

In some cases, the caseworkers will recommend that children be placed in temporary foster homes until such time as it is safe for them to return home. This alternative is usually a last resort, used when a mother is believed to be unprotective or abusive toward the child. In Washington state (and many other states), police or sheriff's department representatives must be involved in the removal and temporary placement of children.

(4) **When child is temporarily removed.** The CPS worker may recommend foster care up to 72 hours (three days), in situations where this is deemed to be the best protection for the child. During this time, CPS must either recommend that the child be returned to the "custodial parent(s)" or must file a "dependency petition." The purpose of this 72-hour period is to allow sufficient time for a police investigation into the allegations and for a more definitive recommendation to be formulated regarding the child's custody.

(5) **Police (or sheriff) investigate the allegations.** It is the responsibility of law enforcement officials in the jurisdiction where the incest occurred to investigate allegations. This will entail a police or sheriff's officer interviewing the child, other parties significant to the case (e.g., teachers, mother, CPS caseworker), and the offender. Some police and sheriffs' departments, as well as prosecutors' offices, now use trained "child interviewers" to gather facts from the child. Some departments have a representative of the prosecutor's office and police department present together in order to lessen the need for children to make their statement more than once. Prosecutors and others (sometimes including mothers) often may view the child's interview through a one-way glass.

You may want to have a legal advocate with you during this procedure to help support you and your child and explain what is happening.

(6) **You may request a shelter care hearing.** Also called a "three-day hearing," (see #4, above), this event is a civil action held before a juvenile court judge sometime within the first 72 hours after a child is removed from its home and placed in foster care. By law in Washington state, a judge must return a child to its "custodial par-

ents" within three days unless the state can prove that the child's release would present a serious threat of substantial harm to that child. It is usually the CPS caseworkers who explain what this danger is and why the child should remain in foster care (if this is the recommendation).

(7) **The suspected offender will be interviewed by police and may be arrested.** If police and/or court believe he is unlikely to flee, he may be arrested and then released.

At this stage, the offender may deny the child's accusations. Or he may make a voluntary confession of his sexual abuse of the child(ren) involved. If he makes a full disclosure, he can eliminate the need for a trial and the need for the child, himself and others to testify in court. A confession also minimizes the degree to which the abuse will be public—often an appealing aspect of confession for offenders who prefer to operate in an atmosphere of secrecy. (In communities where prosecutors are more likely to prosecute sexual abuse cases on the basis of children's statements, there are higher rates of voluntary confessions and guilty pleas by offenders.)

(8) **The prosecutor will file charges; suspect will be arraigned.** In cases where the offender does not make a voluntary confession, a prosecutor will file documents informing the suspect of charges against him, and the court will schedule an arraignment within two weeks. The defendant must appear at arraignment and enter a plea of not guilty. The defendant is typically represented by an attorney in these and subsequent stages. (Offenders who avoided the court process by making a confession may be sentenced within a few weeks [6-8 in Washington state], and may be able to be recommended for treatment for their offenses.) Offenders who deny the child's allegations and plead not guilty can usually expect to face trial for criminal charges.

(9) **Pretrial hearings may be held.** You and your child will not likely be present at any pretrial hearings that might occur in superior court prior to the time of the official trial. These events are for prosecuting attorney and defendant's attorney to file documents and negotiate details related to the official trial.

**(10) Dependency fact-finding hearing is held.** Also called the "45-day hearing," this is a second hearing held in cases in which the juvenile judge has determined the child should remain in foster care beyond the initial 72 hours.

Your child may be represented by a Guardian Ad Litem (an independent citizen advocate) in these proceedings and you are entitled to legal counsel (i.e., an attorney) appointed by the state attorney general's office. You may ask your legal advocate about how to obtain these additional support services.

The dependency fact-finding hearing also takes place in juvenile court and is a civil action. The purpose of this hearing is to decide if incest has occurred, and whether the child should remain in long-term protective care or returned home. Although this is a formal hearing before a judge, attorneys for both the state and the defendant are present, and witnesses testify under oath, this hearing should not be confused with the criminal trial that decides the offender's (defendant's) guilt or innocence that will come later (see below).

**(11) Case goes to criminal trial.** In instances when the accused offender denies he has committed the sexual abuse, he will stand trial for charges brought against him by the state attorney. This trial will be held in superior court in the jurisdiction where the incest occurred.

The prosecuting attorney handling your child's case is likely to talk with you and the child on one or more occasions in advance of the trial. These meetings are for the prosecutor to gain more detail about the allegations of abuse and to prepare you and your child for testimony and other court procedures. You may ask any questions you have about what will happen at the trial at these meetings, including whether or not you and your child will be called to testify. The prosecuting attorney should show the child the court room and explain what will happen during the trial.

You may want your legal advocate to accompany you to these advance meetings, as well as to the trial, for support and help to you interpret what is happening legally. You and your child will only be required to be present in the courtroom during the time you testify.

(12) **The convicted offender will be sentenced.** Several weeks after the conviction, the judge who conducted the trial will announce the offender's sentence. You and your child are encouraged to submit letters to the judge in advance of this event, stating the impact that the offender's abuse has had on your lives. You may also be present at the sentencing.

## SEQUENCE OF EVENTS IN MOLESTATION CASES

The events described above are also relevant to cases involving nonfamilial sexual abuse, except for those related to removal of the offender or child from the home and the various hearings related to child custody.

## PARENTS' RIGHTS IN THE LEGAL PROCESS

You have certain specific and implied rights in legal procedures associated with your child's molestation or incest case. These include:
(1) **Information.** You have the right to ask CPS, police, prosecutor, and others to explain the status of your case, when events will occur, and other things not clear to you. You are also entitled to an advocate to assist you in gathering information (and provide other needed support).
(2) **Files.** You have the right to see your CPS files.
(3) **Confidentiality.** You have the right to expect agency and court information about your (and your child's) private life to be kept confidential, except for details specifically related to the incest or molestation. Further, you will find it helpful to know that most (but not all) news media have a policy of not disclosing the names of victims of sexual abuses. They do, however, sometimes publish the names of suspected and convicted offenders.
(4) **Contact with child in foster care.** You have the right to have contact with your child during the time she or he is in foster care, unless a judge has specifically forbidden contact. Your child may also call home to talk with family members, and visits may be

arranged between the child and you (and other family members) through the CPS caseworkers.

## CIVIL SUITS AGAINST OFFENDERS

Civil suits have become widely used by victims (and their families) of sexual abuse to seek justice against offenders. Civil suits differ from criminal cases in significant ways. First, civil suits seek monetary or property compensation from offenders, rather than treatment or punishment. Second, civil suits may be filed even in cases where there has not been a criminal proceeding. Third, civil suits also may be filed in cases where there has already been a criminal prosecution. In fact, a conviction should strengthen your civil case. Filing a successful civil suit requires an attorney who is familiar with these kinds of cases and, if possible, has a proven track record.

The down side to civil cases is that they may be dragged out for months and years. Prolonging an outcome (and wearing down your will to carry on) is often a strategy of offenders' attorneys. You should prepare yourself for this by establishing a long-term support network.

On the other hand, victims are winning their cases in courts throughout the U.S. For these winners, the effort of filing a civil suit is clearly worthwhile. But even those whose cases are not victorious sometimes convey a sense of personal strength gained during the process. As some note, the transition from victim to survivor can lie in the very act of standing up for ourselves and taking the system as far as we can to find justice.

Communication helps to heal both mother and child.
*Photo: C. Mendoza*

# 5.

# Parenting Issues

## INTRODUCTION

Earlier sections of this book stressed the importance of believing and supporting children who disclose incest, of building strong trust and emotional bonds between mother and child, and of establishing an atmosphere of "no secrets" in your household.

This section will concentrate on some of the questions that mothers frequently ask regarding the parenting of their children once a child has been sexually molested. The answers that follow are brief. You may want to read more extensively on some of these issues.

## COMMONLY ASKED QUESTIONS

**Was this my child's fault?** No, it wasn't. The child is not responsible for what someone else has done to her/him.

**Does my child need counseling?** Yes, by someone trained to work with sexually abused children. This is particularly true for children who were molested repeatedly by one or more offenders.

**How will the molestation affect my child?** Children do not all react in the same ways. Your child's response to the molestation will depend on many factors, including his/her age, knowledge of sexuality and abuse, and the kind and frequency of the abusive act, among other things. While it is difficult to generalize, the child who is nonviolently molested once may not suffer as serious emotional harm as the child who is raped or molested under threats or use of violence, or is repeatedly molested over a period of time. Some predictable reactions in young children are instances of sexual acting out (e.g., frequently touching their genitals or trying to touch someone else's, undressing at inappropriate times), changes in appetite, sleep disturbances, regressive behavior (e.g., bed-wetting or thumb-sucking), unexplainable fears, confusion or disorientation, withdrawal or depression, or angry acting out. Children may also exhibit a lack of trust toward others and not want you to leave them with another person, particularly a stranger. Both younger and older children trapped in incestuous abuse say the incest made them feel bad about themselves; this can result in low self-esteem and low motivation.

**Did the child enjoy the sex?** Violent sexual acts like rape are not pleasurable, nor are most acts committed once against a child. Children molested repeatedly over a period of time do sometimes experience pleasure from the sexual stimulation. It is normal to feel good during sex, but it is abusive when this experience is imposed on a child. Again, remember that it is not the child's fault this happened.

**Why is my child so angry at me?** Your child may have expected you to know she/he was molested or to have prevented it from happening. The child may have put out indirect "messages" to tell you and expected you to read them—this is what angry acting out or, its reverse, withdrawal, are often about. In situations where children are being molested by a family member (or another person who has regular access to the child), the child may have wondered if you knew and approved of what was happening. Or, the child may have believed the lies the offender told her/him about you so the child would dislike you (and develop loyalty and vulnerability to him). Anger can be alleviated with counseling and a commitment to unconditional love on your part. By not blaming your child, and by giving consistent support and guidance, you will further encourage her/him to let go of anger.

**Has my child contracted venereal or other diseases, or developed other medical problems because of the sex?** Only a checkup by a sensitive physician will tell for sure. Children of all ages generally need to be reassured that their bodies are all right after they are molested. A medical exam and lab tests can answer your (and the child's) concerns. Make sure the physician understands the child has been abused and does only the required medical procedures. Increasing numbers of physicians are trained in sexual abuse and how to work with young victims.

**How will the molestation affect my other children?** The other children may feel different from the child who was abused and perhaps begin to act distant, jealous (because the victim sibling is getting so much attention now), or otherwise differently than before. Depending on the age and knowledge of the other children, they may also exhibit confusion over what is happening. If they are very young, they may not grasp *what* has happened, even if you explain. If they strongly identify and empathize with the victim sibling, they may exhibit traumatic responses similar to the victim. Talking to your children and giving them factual information is important. Keep them updated as new events occur to help them understand why so much attention is focused on their sibling. Explain that your child (the victim) will be okay and that they should be especially kind to each other right now.

**Will my child have sexual "hang-ups?"** Your child may have a lot of feelings and fears about sex that most children her/his age do not. A good counselor can help to open discussions about sexuality and other problems that presently exist (or that surface later on). You can help your child by reinforcing the notion that sexual experiences can be positive and healthy, especially when they are more mature. Adolescents emerging from incest experiences are already highly sexualized and may seek sexual encounters outside the family. In this case, you may want to initiate discussions with your child about how to take responsibility and protect herself against disease and unwanted pregnancy. Some children grow up with a fear of or aversion to sex—one of the unfortunate forms of damage sometimes done by incestuous abuse.

**How much should we talk about the molestation?** The molestation will probably take center stage at your house in the beginning. It may be a constant source of spoken and unspoken concern for days or weeks. You will need to talk about the incident(s) as the need arises and as often as it is an obvious topic of concern. Over time it will probably fade as the most immediate problem. But even then, it may linger, shadowing events and the discussions of family members. Play it by ear. Ask your children if they think it is being talked about too much, if this is your worry.

**Is there anyone outside the family we should tell about the molestation?** Teachers and anyone else who has regular contact with your child will find it helpful to know the child has been abused. You can ask these people to respect your and your child's privacy by not telling others, if you want. Beyond these essential people, it is you and your child's decision who should be told. Make sure every member of the family is aware of who should and should not be given the information.

**Will our family ever normal and happy again?** Yes, and you can contribute to it happening. Begin to maintain regular household routines as soon as possible (schedules, chores, celebrations). Maintain discipline guidelines. Praise and reward your children when appropriate. Be consistent with rules and praise. Institute times for reaction. Work on communicating often and honestly.

The following questions arise particularly among mothers whose children were incestuously abused:

**Why do I feel jealous toward my daughter?** Probably because you have come to see your child as a competitor for your husband's (or partner's) affection. Or you feel that because he chose her, she is more attractive than you. Again, remember that she is a child, and she may have been very young and vulnerable when all this began. Also, it serves the offender's motives to have you and your daughter at odds. She is much more likely to side with him if you distance yourself from her or behave jealously. Jealousy is a common reaction for mothers and can be worked through, with the aid of a counselor and your commitment to understand what has happened.

**Can my daughter and husband have a normal relationship again?** Well, they have not *really* had a normal father-daughter relationship since he first fantasized having sex with her. They can establish a *new* relationship with some strict ground rules, long-term counseling, and a commitment on each of their parts to enter into a new relationship. Some father-daughter relationships are permanently impaired, however, and not able to be salvaged.

How do we establish trust and openness in our family? By expressing your thoughts and feelings with your children and encouraging them to do the same. By sharing the things you did that day. By taking time to listen to them. Start in small ways—share the things you are most comfortable with and move on from there. Be consistent in trying, even if you don't see immediate results. Incestuous family members have typically learned to keep secrets from one another; the household may be a context for tension and isolation for everyone. It's time to break down the lack of communication, beginning with an honesty around what has happened. Bring your children into family decision-making whenever possible. Observe respect and boundaries with each other.

## WHY CHILD MOLESTATION SHOULD BE REPORTED

Child molestation should be reported to authorities for several reasons. First, to protect your child and other children from further abuse. Second to make a statement to your child that what has happened to her/him is very serious, must be stopped, and that the offender must be punished (or helped through therapy). Third, to require police, courts and other social agencies to be responsible for stopping child sexual abuse.

The matter of treatment is especially important. Very few child molesters (or other sex offenders) will seek or remain in treatment programs voluntarily. For this reason it is essential that the offender is evaluated by a competent psychologist trained to treat and assess sex offenders and then, if found treatable, to be monitored regularly regarding his progress. None of us, as private citizens, has the power or authority to do these things—only the legal system does.

You may find it awkward and traumatic to report your child's molestation, particularly if the offender is a relative or someone else you know. If the offender was your husband or another child in the family, you may be torn by confusion and competing feelings of love and loyalty. You may be weighed down by the thought of sending someone to jail or prison, or fearful of what publicity will do to your family. Some mothers dread the possibility of violent retaliation by the offender, particularly if he has already been abusive to her and the children.

These (and other concerns of yours) are valid. Reporting child molestation involves risks. There is way to know exactly how it will turn out, no guarantee that the criminal justice system or "helping professionals" along the way are going to be sensitive, completely fair, or altogether competent. The reasons for reporting remain strong, however, and confront each mother whose child has been molested. As more and more cases of incest and other child molestation have been reported these last 10-15 years, our social institutions have been increasingly adept at and responsible for handling the problems effectively and treating the victims and families with respect.

# 6.

# Cultural Issues

## INTRODUCTION

The abuse of women and children in many ethnic communities has been much less visible than in white communities in the U.S. these last two decades. Even as the issues of sexual abuse became major public concerns and reporting doubled and tripled through the years, many mothers of color have been reluctant to report and seek help for themselves and their children through the criminal justice system, rape crisis centers and other agencies. In exploring some of the reasons this has been true, I use the term "mothers of color" to refer to women who are not white, western European by heritage.

This chapter also identifies some of the survival tactics that have worked for mothers of color, as well as suggestions for greater responsiveness on the part of police, court, and various agency personnel. The information here has been drawn from real life stories of mothers of color, from women of color working in community agencies, and from published first-person articles by women of color.

## HISTORICAL AND CULTURAL PATTERNS

Even before the civil rights movement of the 1960s brought renewed attention to race relations among the general public, the awareness was etched clearly in the minds of large communities of people in the U.S. To be Native American, African-American, or of Asian, South Pacific, Latin or other non-western European descent often meant a separate reality for millions. One feature of that reality has historically been exclusion from the same benefits, privileges and protections enjoyed by the white majority culture. Another all too common feature has been physical, economic, and psychological injury to people and communities of color.

Attitudes and practices in the majority culture are still slow to change; only consistent pressure by civil rights groups, new laws and (court interpretations of them), education, and individual challenges to discrimination have brought improvements.

Any mother who learns her child has been molested has a difficult ordeal before her, as earlier chapters discuss. Mothers of color may have additional challenges and barriers to address and hurdle. Some of the problems mothers of color confront may be in their own communities, where many have confronted a pervasive silence around rape, molestation, incest and family violence. Cultural values also have sometimes made it difficult for victims to seek help.

But it is the larger society and its agencies that will most likely offer the greater obstacles. Police, prosecutors, judges, and helping professionals are still a mostly white group operating on the beliefs, norms, and rules of a racist society. And mistrust of these systems have generated fear of speaking out and reporting on the part of victims and mothers of color. There are, of course, examples of enlightenment out there, both at the individual and agency levels. These examples—agencies with ethnically-diverse staffs and/or staffs generally trained to be sensitive to the needs of ethnically-diverse peoples—provide greater hope for mothers of color who decide to report their children's abuse and follow through with prosecution, counseling, and other services.

The big picture is a troubling one, however. Statistics show a U.S. deeply divided along racial lines. For instance, while about a fourth of African-Americans today fall into middle-class categories, most live significantly below poverty lines. Disproportionate numbers of other non-white people also live in poverty, occupy jails and prisons, and live on the streets. Infant mortality rates are nearly double for non-white, inner city populations. Non-white males are brutalized by police more much more often than their white male counterparts. And so forth. These are some of the hard facts that shape many mothers' perceptions of the larger society and affect their decisions about how and whether to approach legal and other agencies when their children are molested.

Many reminders that the "system" may not be there in the same way for mothers of color as they are for caucasian members of society are more subtle, however, as the following story illustrates.

## ONE WOMAN'S STORY: YOLANDA

Yolanda sat with her two daughters across the table from the child protective services worker. Yolanda had left her job early to make the appointment on time. Her daughters, 7 and 10, had been brought directly from school by their neighbor Charlotte. This was the day the girls were going to tell "what happened" when their father allegedly molested them on three separate nights while Yolanda was working.

Yolanda was afraid that her daughters would be taken away by the CPS worker. She worried they might be put into a foster home where she couldn't see them and where the foster family wouldn't understand their culture. She feared what her parents and brothers and sister were going to say when they found out she had told someone outside the family about the incest. She wondered what would happen to her husband Pedro, who was still a legal citizen of Mexico. She spoke good English and had recently become a U.S. citizen herself, but she still didn't understand all of the laws and procedures that seemed to control their lives right now. She only felt sure that Pedro had to be stopped from ever hurting her girls again.

The CPS worker, a blonde woman in her thirties, directed her questions to Charlotte. Charlotte then turned to the girls or Yolanda and repeated the question, as if they hadn't understood. This seemed odd to Yolanda, especially since her daughters' first language was English. She thought Charlotte was behaving strange and uncharacteristic of her usual friendly self. The interview, which went on for nearly an hour, was frustrating for everyone. Yolanda felt tears spill down her face at the end. Then the CPS worker explained that the police would have to interview the girls again, separately, to get the official statement. She did not explain what would happen to her girls or to Pedro.

Yolanda went away without many of her questions and concerns answered. She was self-conscious about her accent and afraid to speak to the CPS worker, who rarely looked at her. She had felt invisible, powerless, and insignificant. She felt embarrassed to be so humiliated before her daughters. When she heard the details of the incest, she felt desolate and alone. She wished for someone to talk to.

## A MORE HELPFUL APPROACH

There are several ways that this real-life story might have been different. The CPS worker might have inquired in advance of the meeting if Yolanda wanted a rape crisis advocate to provide emotional support and explain both relevant laws and agencies' procedures. The CPS worker might have even assisted Yolanda in calling the rape crisis center to locate an a Hispanic advocate (or one familiar with the Hispanic cultures) who could provide Yolanda with basic information on laws and available services in the Spanish-speaking community.

At the beginning of the interview, the CPS worker might have clearly explained the purpose of today's meeting and what would happen next. She might have spoken directly with Yolanda and her daughters, recognizing that their lives (not Charlotte's) were impacted by the incest. She might have asked if Yolanda or the girls had any questions before they left. Charlotte might have tactfully bowed out of the intermediate role she came to occupy. Rather than ally herself with the CPS worker, Charlotte might have indicated that she was there for Yolanda and the girls' support.

With the encouragement of a co-worker, Yolanda did contact the local rape crisis center later that night and discussed her experience at the CPS office with an advocate. The advocate, a white woman in her twenties, who had familiarity with the Mexican-American culture from communities where she had lived in California, was able to affirm Yolanda's reasons for distress and to provide some support. She was able to answer many of Yolanda's basic questions about the investigation process and what might happen with the girls and her husband. She later helped Yolanda locate a therapist in a nearby town who was able to counsel the children. (Local police located Pedro nearly two weeks later and returned him to Mexico, something Yolanda had feared.)

## SURVIVAL ISSUES FOR MOTHERS OF COLOR

It is difficult to generalize about the experiences of women of color whose children have been molested. Each distinct cultural group has its own range of values, traditions, stories, and healing systems. In addition, a mother's educational level, socio-economic status, and experiences interacting with public agencies may affect how she responds to her child's molestation. In addition, some mothers of color identify more closely with the traditional beliefs and practices of their cultural groups than others.

What follows are some more common issues (and ways of responding) that arise for mothers when their children are molested.

**Taboos.** Mothers sometimes encounter an entrenched cultural taboo against revealing that incest or molestation have happened in the family. There may even be a system of punishment (e.g., shaming, shunning or banning by the community) for those who break the taboo by reporting to police or talking to counselors. Some taboos are very extensive, forbidding the disclosure of any personal problem, especially one relating to sexual matters or defeat. Women who belong to immigrant communities may be more profoundly silenced by such taboos than those who have encountered resistance or outright disobedience to them among second and later generation women. Increasing numbers of women of color are speaking out about child molestation and other assault, perhaps agreeing with African-American writer Audre Lorde's remark that "the speaking profits me, beyond any other effect."

**Traditions.** Beliefs and customs (religious and otherwise) vary from one cultural group to the next. Like Yolanda, you may be poignantly aware of this as you enter the world of legal and social service systems and encounter people who are unfamiliar with your values, ways of behaving, and even dressing. What parts of your traditions do you hold dear? Which traditions and ways give you strength, identity in a crisis like this? Which aspects of your traditions make it difficult for you to understand, accept, or speak about what has happened?

**Prejudice and stereotypes.** These are probably not new problems to you, but they can make your already difficult situation even more painful and frustrating. Some women have addressed instances of prejudice against them (or their children) by conveying to agency personnel that their behavior is unacceptable or offensive. You have the right to expect fair treatment and even to complain if you don't get it.

**The criminal "justice" system.** For many years mothers of color have been reluctant to report child molestation (and other violence) by members of their own communities for fear they will get the runaround, that police and prosecutors will give less attention to their cases, and that offenders will receive harsher treatment under the white-dominated justice system. These are possibilities, thus a real dilemma for you—but a dilemma that should be tempered by the knowledge that he may harm your child (or others) again. Some mothers of color say it helped them to remember that "his crime against my child" was causing this ordeal and that the risks and uncertainties seemed worth it. An adept legal advocate (from a rape crisis center or other community group) can support you through the system and help see that you and your children receive the attention coming to you.

**Counseling and helping services.** There is nothing wrong with asking agencies you have to deal with if there is someone on staff who is from your ethnic background, or who is familiar with your culture. You are also free to "shop around," once someone is assigned to you—if you don't feel comfortable with the first person, inquire about who else is available. Though this may seem awkward, most agencies are used to it and may want to show they are trying their best to serve a diverse clientele.

**Laws and rights.** You should get a clear reading on the state and federal laws and policies that pertain specifically to you and your case as soon as possible after your child discloses. There may be lawyers, civil rights, or other advocacy groups who can be helpful to you at this point. Mothers facing immigration concerns will need legal assistance relevant to her particular issues.

**Language barriers.** Immigrant mothers may need an interpreter to help her interact with the legal and helping service personnel. "Language banks" are available in many areas where Southeast Asian, Hispanic, and other international communities have settled. One problem that has sometimes arisen when using interpreters from the mother's own community, however, is that the information is then passed along to others. Safety for the mother and children from the offender should be a vital concern for those making interpreter arrangements.

**Other people's expectations.** Many mothers of color are pulled by competing loyalties when their children are abused. Families, churches, friends, children all need you and want you to do more than perhaps you feel you can. One mother made a list of what different people had asked "suggested" she do or demanded of her. Next to each she listed reasons she did or didn't want to respond. In this way, she clarified what she expected of herself.

**A sense of family.** Many cultures stress the wholeness of families and the importance of sticking together in hard times. When a family is divided by crisis, particularly incest, a mother may feel unable to keep this value intact. With the offender gone, mothers are able to reunite and strengthen bonds with her children and her side of the family. It may not be so easy with the offender's family, however. On the other hand, mothers whose children are molested by a non-family member often find their families enormously helpful, in terms of emotional support and helping with child care, in this time of crisis.

**Shame.** In many cultures, shame is an important element of social control. One may be supposed to avoid bringing shame upon oneself, the family, and/or community by avoiding certain things—like talking about personal problems. For many, shame is accompanied by severe personal consequences, such as banishment from the community. Many women who feel ashamed grow depressed. In some traditional communities women have been talking among themselves about personal matters as a way of alleviating the anxiety of carrying a personal burden (like the knowledge your child has been molested).

## THE STRENGTH OF HERITAGE

Many women of color find great strength in their heritage in this time of crisis. Is there something in your culture that provides a source of pride, comfort, encouragement, and hope at this time? Is there a story common to your family or culture that helps explain or resolve what has happened, or suggest a path for you to follow? Are there identified healers, leaders, social workers, counselors or others to whom you can go for encouragement and support? Many ethnic communities recognize the prevalence of sexual abuse (and other problems of violence) and have established services for community members. You may want to see what is available in your area.

## 7.

# Common Religious Issues Surrounding Molestation

## By Rev. Joan B. Ham*

*It is not an enemy who taunts me—*
   *then I could bear it;*
*It is not an adversary who deals insolently with me—*
   *then I could hide from him.*
*But it is you, my equal, my companion,*
   *my familiar friend.*
*We used to hold sweet converse together;*
   *within God's house we walked in fellowship.*
                    (Psalm 55: 12-14)

Throughout the crisis of disclosure and the time you are beginning to put things back together, you will probably find that you feel there is nothing in your life left unaffected. If you are a woman of faith, you may discover religious issues and questions arising out of your experi-

* Rev. Joan Ham has worked as a volunteer sexual assault counselor and served on the board of a women's shelter in the state of Colorado. She is presently serving as pastor at the Cathlamet Congregational United Church of Christ and the Skamokawa Community United Methodist church, both in southwest Washington state.

ence. At this time, some mothers use their faith as a natural help. Others live through a crisis and transformation of faith in addition to everything else that is changing. Whether religious beliefs provide stability or more upheaval at this time, this section is here to highlight some of the religious issues which come as a result of the molestation. It is written from the perspective of a "mainline, Judeo-Christian" heritage. The author recognizes the limitations of that tradition, as well as the fact that other religious communities may also offer their own unique resources for you at this time.

Religious issues and questions come at a lot of different times in our lives. When they occur at times of crisis, we find ourselves alienated from that power which might otherwise be a resource of strength and courage. To find our faith in question in times of trouble not only can be frightening, it can heighten our sense of crisis and feeling of being out of control.

## BETRAYAL

Feeling betrayal by an intimate friend, lover, or family member is only part of the crisis. You may also echo the sentiments of another psalm, "My God, my God, why have you forsaken me?" (Psalm 22:1). What kind of God could possibly have let this happen to my daughter, or to me? We depend upon God to protect and love that which God has created. Now you may feel that trust has been violated not only for yourself, but also for those you love and wish to protect. Anger at what is perceived as a new level of victimization and betrayal is a normal response.

Jesus quoted this psalm from the cross. It is helpful to remember that this use of a psalm which gave words to the feelings he was experiencing did not place him outside of God's love, nor did it stop the work of God that was taking place. It is not that God wills for you to be in this crisis, but that your anger will not stop God's care for you at this time. Your faith may very well be strong enough to withstand your anger.

## GUILT

The question, "What kind of God is this?" has its human sequel in the question, "What kind of person am I?" There are a host of questions and statements around the issue of guilt that you might be feeling and thinking.

— How could I have let this happen?
— Why didn't I know?
— How can I feel jealous?
— I'm *so* angry!
— I hate him/her/myself!

These are the kinds of thoughts which are so often classified as "unfaithful" or "irreligious" and we feel even more guilt for even thinking about them. That only serves to make one feel more alienated.

A valuable resource at this point is the first creation account in Genesis. It states that men and women were both created by God, and that creation was pronounced "good" by the Creator (Genesis 1:27-31). While we lose confidence in ourselves and others, God's confidence in us does not fail. You, as a mother, were not responsible for the molestation. Be gentle with yourself on the issue of self-blame. You will need that energy to respond to other needs for yourself and your family.

## FORGIVENESS

The issue of guilt raises also the question of forgiveness. The responsibility for the molestation lies with the offender. When/how do you forgive him?

For Christians, forgiving is one means of letting go and disarming the power that the offense has over a victim's life. Jesus teaches that a person must be willing to confront the offense and be willing to forgive as many times as it takes. But it is also clear in this scripture that a person's forgiveness is dependent on the offender's repentance (and, we should add, the willingness to take responsibility for the harm he has done). Forgiveness does not just happen, nor is it unconditional. It occurs within a context in which the victim has made the conscious choice to forgive (thereby letting go of the pain and anger). As a result, the victim will feel empowered through God's grace and will experience a sense of justice.

Most important, forgiveness happens in its own time and cannot be rushed. It may take one year or thirty. Pastors or counselors can be present to a victim as she/he struggles with the need and desire to forgive, but the work and process of forgiveness lies within the victim her/himself.

## GRIEF

The last issue to be highlighted here is that of grief. The changes that occur in the family as a result of the molestation, and the pain you feel for your child(ren) and yourself, set in motion all the dynamics of grief. The words of God spoken through the prophet Jeremiah reflect the level of God over a broken covenant. Similarly you may feel the same grief and rejection.

> *My grief is beyond healing,*
> *my heart is sick within me.*
> *Hark the cry of the daughter of my people*
> *from the length and breadth of the land;*
> *Is not the Lord in Zion?*
> *Is her king not in her?*
> ♦ ♦ ♦ ♦ ♦ ♦ ♦
> *Because of the wound of the daughter of my people*
> *am I wounded.*
> *I mourn, and dismay has taken hold of me.*
> *Is there no balm in Gilead? Is there no physician there?*
> *Why is there no healing for the daughter*
> *of my people?*
> *O that my head were waters,*
> *my eyes a fountain of tears,*
> *that I might weep day and night for the slain*
> *of the daughter of my people!*
>                              (Jeremiah 8:19-9:1)

You may weep for the loss of the old and not be able to see what is new. You may cry for your child's pain, and wonder if things will ever be right again. Jeremiah, in later chapters, goes on to speak of new hope and promises which are not based on the old ones. You and your child(ren) will also begin to see new hopes and promises in time. They may or may not include the family in the way you have known it. This period of intense crisis and grief will pass and a new time will come.

The list of religious issues and resources here is far from complete. Written faith stories and resources help to reassure us as well as provide us a reflection and validation of our innermost thoughts. Ultimately, the embodiment of these resources within the community of faith is far more helpful. People who are willing to listen to your story and share in some way in healing and beginning a new story may be the best help you can find.

## A ROLE FOR CLERGY

Faith communities have long proclaimed themselves as a haven for those who are battered by life. As helpful as that sounds, it must be noted that religious communities, in general, have not acknowledged sexual violence, particularly incest, as a reality in their midst. Clergy have in the past, and some in the present, maintained a trick response along the lines of, "Go home and pray about it." Unfortunately, if you are faced with serious questions and issues in your faith because of incest in your family, simplistic, trivial answers are not resources for you.

Check with your local CPS worker, rape crisis counselors, and with friends. The chances are someone will know of religious leaders in the area who will take the time to listen and offer help and support to you through this time. Some women will return to a clergy person who has not been helpful, perhaps thinking, "If I explain it again, perhaps s/he will listen and understand this time." If a religious leader is not helpful (will not listen, blames you, or minimizes the problem in any way), do not go back. This is not a time for you to feel any less in control, or less capable as a human being. It is a time for strengthening and healing, and there are religious resources, both people and traditions, to aid that process.

# 8.

# Issues in Mothers' Recovery

## by Muriel Templeton, M.S. *

## INTRODUCTION

Counseling services for offenders and victims have developed over the years and have become reasonably available in many communities. However, the needs of the nonoffending spouses and other family members are seldom offered or met beyond the initial time of disclosure and involvement with the official agencies.

Mothers of sexually molested children often say they feel like "mother-in-the-middle"—inadequate to meet everyone else's needs, neglected by those they love and the agencies they have to deal with, and troubled by many unresolved conflicts and issues.

## COUNSELING ISSUES

While each mother brings her own unique problems and questions into counseling, several common concerns emerge.

* Muriel Templeton, M.S., is a certified mental health counselor in the State of Washington. She has been working with survivors and families affected by sexual assault and family violence for twenty years.

*Children's blame and anger.* I have found that when mothers are given the opportunity to deal with their own issues in counseling that, quite often, the first feeling to emerge is their resentment and confusion over the *blame* and *anger* directed at them by their daughter or son. It seems that children expect mothers to be able to read minds, to know what is going on without being told. The child may have given a mother vague, indirect messages that all is not well, but only with hindsight can a mother usually "read" the hidden truth of what was going on.

Sometimes it is useful to schedule some joint mother-daughter (or son) sessions, to allow the daughter to express her anger, have it redirected appropriately, and to lay the foundation to prepare for a new way of communicating between mother and child. Children's extreme anger can often be disconcerting for mothers, particularly if mothers have difficulty expressing their own anger. Joint counseling can become a place where mothers and children both learn to articulate angry feelings and to direct them at the offender who has caused their pain.

*Mother-child alienation.* Very often, especially in cases of incest, alienation develops between a mother and daughter (or son). This is usually something that has been manipulated by the father or stepfather to facilitate the ongoing abuse. Mothers can use counseling as a place to explore the way this alienation came about and to consider ways of overcoming it. This often becomes an opportunity for mothers and daughters, in particular, to develop a new kind of relationship that will last and enhance the rest of their lives.

*Adolescent victim behavior and loyalty toward the offender.* In cases of incest, mothers often report their helplessness and confusion when their adolescent daughter begins to act out in a self-destructive way after the disclosure and legal intervention.

Truancy, running away, staying out at night, sexual involvement with older men and strangers, and drug and alcohol abuse are common behaviors with adolescent incest victims. Mothers, already feeling guilty, often become desperate about their inability to protect their daughters from further harm.

I believe it is important to help mothers to recognize that adolescents, in particular, still feel a loyalty towards their family member abuser. They are affected by their perceived "participation" in the sexual abuse. This confusion results in lack of feelings of self-worth and leads to self-destructive "exciting" behaviors. An understanding of these issues will help the mother to be more supportive toward her daughter rather than rejecting. It can be helpful to work on ways of developing protective limits for the daughter, possibly in cooperation with school personnel in counseling sessions.

*Mothers' own victimization.* Mothers are often confronted with the need to deal with their own prior sexual victimization after their children are sexually abused. Hearing the child's story may cause a mother to remember her own molestation or incest and to re-experience the anguish, guilt, and other feelings associated with it. Mothers who have never told anyone about their victimization may be reluctant to do so now, when they feel their job is to comfort their children. In addition, they have spent many years internalizing the shame and self-blame while they have kept the secret of their sexual abuse.

All mothers I have known have found dealing with their own abuse to be a basic starting point in counseling. Once they have talked about their own victimization they are free from their guilt and emotional trauma and able to be more responsive to their own children. Most women make immediate connections between their past victimization and events in their current lives, once they explore these issues. One such link may be their vulnerability to continued manipulation or abuse by their husbands or partners. Finding ways to deal with current, related problems is made possible through the retrospective work.

## SELECTING A COUNSELOR

You should begin your own counseling experience knowing that you are the expert on your situation. Counselors can help you clarify your problems and support you in making choices, and they can guide you toward more knowledge of child molestation. But, in the end, no one will know more than you do about your life, your thoughts and feelings than you do. You can remain secure in this fact through your counseling.

For these and other reasons, most mothers find either short-term or long-term counseling a necessary part of surviving their child's molestation. Some mothers have had previous experience working with counselors; others are entering the counseling experience for the first time. In selecting a counselor, you have the right to work with a counselor who:

— You are comfortable with and feel is trustworthy,
— Respects you and listens to your concerns and feelings,
— Supports your own goals and choices, and will affirm your assertiveness in making important decisions,
— Has adequate experience and training to work with family members hurt by incest or molestation,
— Accepts the offender's responsibility for what has happened,
— And recognizes and supports you as a whole person, including your cultural and religious beliefs, sexual orientation, education, and socioeconomic situation.

You may want to make a mental or written list of questions to ask the counselor during your first session that will help you decide if this is the best person for you. You are free to inquire about the counselor's training, philosophy toward molestation and incest, attitudes toward women, and any other matter that concerns you. If cost is a potential problem for you, you may want to ask about sliding scale fees for clients. These questions are best cleared up *before* the therapy begins. However, you are free to stop seeing a counselor at any point in your therapy if you feel uncomfortable with the person you are seeing.

Your local sexual assault center should have a list of therapists in your area, along with their qualifications, to aid you in finding a counselor.

## STORIES OF MOTHERS' RECOVERY

Following are three success stories drawn from my experiences working with mother survivors. The names have been changed and extensive personal details eliminated in order to protect real identities. The stories are shared with clients' permission in order to illustrate the role of counseling in mothers' recovery.

### Story #1: Marg

I was talking to Marg today whose two children, a boy and a girl, were both extensively abused by her husband. The whole family has been in counseling (individual, family, and play therapy) for over two years now. While Marg and her husband divorced the year after the disclosure, they wanted to work together in family therapy for the children's sake. I asked Marg, "When do you think this will all be over?" She said immediately, "Never," but she said it with a sort of lightness and talked with a laugh that brought home to me all the changes that have already happened for her.

Marg was able to accept the events that had occurred in her family. She would never forget about them, and life would never be the same again. But she could go on from here feeling much better about herself and her parenting skills.

In her counseling, Marg had been supported to explore and accept the fact that her own parents had been physically abusive to her. They had been harmful to her emotionally and not provided her with role models for nurturing her own children. She came to see the ways in which her husband was able to alienate her from her daughter, who displaced her in her mother and wife roles without her understanding what was going on.

Marg gained insight into these family dynamics and was able to begin working on healthy role boundaries with her children and husband. She grew into her role as an empowered adult and parent. In counseling she eventually felt safe enough to talk about her own childhood sexual abuse for the first time and how it had affected her sexuality. Marg had left home after high school graduation to get married and had never worked outside the home. Now, with the help of friends' and her counselor's support, she was able to get a job and feel more independent.

### Story #2: Gina

Gina comes from an ethnic and religious background that has strict teachings regarding a mother's role in the family. She believed that she is responsible for keeping the family intact and meeting the needs of everyone in the family. Shock and amazement overwhelmed Gina when a caseworker from the Department of Social and Health Services and a policeman arrived on the doorstep of her comfortable middle-class home to tell her that her daughter had reported being sexually molested by her father.

Gina's immediate response was, "I don't believe it!" This resulted in her 10-year-old daughter's removal from the home and placement in foster care. Only when her husband had moved out of the house was her daughter allowed to return.

Gina felt depressed and completely inadequate to cope alone with the daily demands and activities of her daughter and teen-age son. She agonized over the fact that her daughter had talked to a stranger about her father's abuse instead of telling her. She struggled with her shame, feeling that she had failed not only as a parent but as a partner, excusing her husband's behavior because of her usual tiredness at the end of the day and frequent lack of interest in having sex with him.

Encouraged by her minister and mother, Gina talked to a counselor every week while her husband was in outpatient treatment with a separate therapist. This helped her to understand that she alone could not be responsible for the health and welfare of the family, and that the traditional sex roles and expectations for a woman that she had accepted, in many ways, contributed to her feelings of guilt and inadequacy.

Gina was able to talk about shame and guilt over her child's removal from her care at the very time the daughter needed her most. Gina came to realize that her husband alone was responsible for his behavior; this helped her to gain better understanding of the relationships within the family and to gain some perspective on her initial response to the incest disclosure. She understood that while she chose to work toward forgiveness of her husband's behavior, that this was not the same as excusing the behavior. Her counselor respected her decision to remain with her husband and to work with him to rebuild the family with the help of their extended families. She was able to define new terms for a "healthy" family within these goals.

## Story #3: Shirley

Often the offender, while known to the family, is not a relative. Less often—but increasingly more common—the child is molested by an older child unknown to the victim or her family. This story emphasizes how a mother's still unresolved feelings about her own childhood sexual molestation is triggered by her daughter's abuse.

Shirley's 3-year-old daughter told her one night, during the child's regular bath, that while she was out playing in the apartment complex playground, a big boy she didn't know had told her to take her clothes off. He subsequently touched the child in her private area.

Shirley was shocked, but she maintained a cool attitude and got a few more details from her daughter. As her child spoke to her, Shirley thought of another little girl, herself, who had been abused by her grandfather when she was three. The "touching" in her own childhood had happened on many occasions, and she still felt the shame and helplessness as she now tried to comfort her own little girl.

Shirley had never told anyone about her own abuse. One day, in a discussion with her daughter's therapist, she acknowledged that she too had been a victim. The therapist encouraged her to get her own counselor and work through her early childhood abuse so that she could feel better able to protect her own child and to improve her relationship with her husband. It seemed that there was a tension in her marriage that revolved around their sexual relationship. This had worsened since their daughter's abuse by the child's requests to sleep with them. Shirley was relieved by the therapist's understanding and support, and she soon chose a counselor who was able to help her talk about her childhood molestation and her current fears and concerns.

This helped Shirley to deal with her daughter's abuse and support her daughter in a way to maintain the child's self-esteem and avoid the guilt and confusion that Shirley had endured. Additionally, Shirley felt confident about talking to her husband about her abuse and how it had affected her sexuality; they worked together to improve their sexual relationship.

Mothers who come through their children's molestation intact may be called
<u>mother survivors</u>.
*Photo: C. Mendoza*

# 9.

# Suggested Reading

## GENERAL REFERENCES

Ashley, Sandi (Ed.). *The Missing Voice: Writings by Mothers of Incest Victims*, Kendall/Hunt Publishing Company, 1992.

Burns, Maryviolet C. (Ed.). *The Speaking Profits Us: Violence in the Lives of Women of Color*, Center for the Prevention of Sexual and Domestic Violence (Seattle), 1986.

Berliner, Lucy. "Another option for victims: Civil damage suits," *Journal of Interpersonal Violence*, 1989, 4, 107-109.

Butler, Sandra. *Conspiracy of Silence: The Trauma of Incest*, New Glide, 1978.

Finkelhor, David. *Sexually Victimized Children*, Free Press (Macmillan Company), 1979.

Fortune, Marie. *Sexual Violence: The Unmentionable Sin*, Pilgrim Press, 1983.

Freeman, Lori. *Loving Touches*, Parenting Press, 1986.

Hunter, Mic. *Abused Boys: The Neglected Victims of Sexual Abuse*, Lexington Books, 1990.

MacFarlane, Kee and Jill Waterman (Eds.). *Sexual Abuse of Young Children*, Guilford Press, 1986.

Russell, Diana E. H. *The Secret Trauma: Incest in the lives of girls and women*, Basic Books, 1986.

## FOR CHILDREN

James, Judy. *It's Not Your Fault*, Chase Franklin Press, 1985.
Russell, Pamela. *Do You Have A Secret?* Comp Care Publications, 1986.

# 10.

# Directory of Services in the United States

The following list of rape crisis services may be helpful to you in finding support for your concerns and problems. This is not a complete list of available services but rather a list to help you locate an agency in your area. Write or call the agency nearest you for a referral.

## ALABAMA
*Council Against Rape/Lighthouse*, 830 S. Court St., Montgomery 36104. (205) 264-7273.
*Russell Student Health Center*, Box Y, Tuscaloosa 35487. (205) 348-6262.

## ALASKA
*Women in Crisis—Counseling and Assistance, Inc.*, 902 Tenth Ave., Fairbanks 99701. (907) 452-7273 or 452-2293.
*Standing Together Against Rape (STAR)*, 3710 E. 20th Ave., Anchorage 99508. (907) 276-7273.

## ARIZONA
*The Center Against Sexual Assault*, 2211 E. Highland, Suite 100, Phoenix 85016. (602) 257-8095.
*Tucson Rape Crisis Center*, Box 40306, Tucson 85717. (602) 623-7273.

## ARKANSAS
*West Arkansas Counseling and Guidance Center*, P.O. Box 2887, Station A, Fort Smith 72913. (501) 452-6650.

*Arkansas Department of Health*, 4815 W. Markham, Little Rock 72205.

## CALIFORNIA
*Child Sexual Abuse Treatment Program* (Humbold Family Service Center), 2841 E St., Eureka. (707) 445-6180.

*East Los Angeles Rape Crisis Center*, P.O. Box 63245, Los Angeles 90063. (213) 262-0944 (Bilingual).

*Women's Institute for Mental Health*, San Francisco. (415) 864-2364.

## COLORADO
*Rape Assistance and Awareness Program (RAAP)*, 640 Broadway #112, Denver 80203. (303) 430-5656, 329-0023 (TDD), 329-0031 (Bilingual).

*Ending Violence Effectively*. P.O. Box 18212, Denver 80218. (303) 322-7010.

*Sexual Assault Team*, The Resource Center, Inc., 1129 Colorado Ave., Grand Junction 81501. (303) 243-0190.

## CONNECTICUT
*Sexual Assault Crisis Service*, YWCA, 135 Broad St., Hartford 06105. (203) 522-6666.

*Greater Bridgeport YWCA Rape Crisis Service*, 753 Fairfield Ave., Bridgeport 06604. (203) 333-2233.

## DELAWARE
*Rape Crisis Center of Wilmington*, P.O. Box 9514, Wilmington 19809. (302) 575-1112.

*Support Group for Victims of Sexual Offense (SOS)*, University of Delaware, Laurel Hall, Newark 19716. (302) 451-2226.

## DISTRICT OF COLUMBIA
*DC Rape Crisis Center*, P.O. Box 21005, Washington, D.C. 20009. (202) 333-RAPE.

## FLORIDA

*Rape Treatment Center*, 1611 N.W. 12th Ave., Miami 33136. (305) 549-RAPE.

*Sexual Assault Treatment Center*, 655 W. 8th St., Jacksonville 32203. (904) 355-7273.

*Refuge House/Rape Crisis*, P.O. Box 4356, Tallahassee 32315. (904) 681-2111.

## GEORGIA

*Rape Crisis Center*, Grady Memorial Hospital, 80 Butler St. S.E., Atlanta 30325. (404) 659-7273.

*Augusta Rape Crisis Line*, University Hospital, 1350 Walton Way, Augusta 30910. (404) 724-5200.

## HAWAII

*Sex Abuse Treatment Center*, Kapiolani Medical Center for Women and Children, 1415 Kalakaua Ave., Suite 201, Honolulu 96826. (808) 524-7273.

*Kauai Victim Witness Program*, 4193 Hardy St., Unit 6, Lihue 96766. (808) 245-5388.

## IDAHO

*Rape Crisis Alliance*, 720 W. Washington St., Boise 83702. (208) 345-7273.

*Alternatives to Violence in the Palouse, Inc.*, c/o Women's Center, University of Idaho, Moscow 83843. (208) 883-HELP.

## ILLINOIS

*Rape and Sexual Abuse Care Center*, Box 1154, Southern Illinois University, Edwardsville 62026. (618) 692-2197.

*Women's Services*, Loop YWCA, 37 S. Wabash, 2nd Floor, Chicago 60603. (312) 372-6600.

## INDIANA

*Midtown Mental Health*, 1001 W. 10th St., Indianapolis 46202. (317) 630-7791.

*Sex Offense Services*, 403 E. Madison, South Bend 46624. (219) 234-0061.

## IOWA

*Sexual Assault Intervention Program*, YWCA, 318 5th St. S.E., Cedar Rapids 52401. (319) 363-5490.

*Rape Victim Advocacy Program*, 130 N. Madison St., Iowa City 52242. (319) 338-4800.

## KANSAS

*Wichita Area Sexual Assault Center*, 215 N. St. Francis, Suite #1, Wichita 67202.

*Crisis Center, Inc.*, P.O. Box 1526, Manhattan 66502. (913) 539-2785.

## KENTUCKY

*Lexington Rape Crisis Center*, P.O. Box 1603, Lexington 40592. (606) 253-2511.

*Rape Victim Services/OASIS*, 1316 W. 4th, Owensboro 42301. (502) 926-7273.

## LOUISIANA

*Family Counseling Agency, Inc.*, 1404 Murray St., Alexandria 71301. (318) 445-2022.

*YWCA Rape Crisis Program*, 601 S. Jefferson Davis Pkwy., New Orleans 70119. (504) 483-8888.

## MAINE

*Rape Crisis Center, Inc.*, P.O. Box 1371, Portland 01401. (207) 774-3613.

## MARYLAND

*Sexual Assault Crisis Center*, 1127 West St., Annapolis 21401. (301) 224-1321.

*Baltimore Center for Victims of Sexual Assault*, 1010 St. Paul St., Suite 2A, Baltimore 21202. (301) 366-RAPE.

## MASSACHUSETTS

*Rape Crisis Program*, 1016 Main St., Worcester 01603. (617) 799-5700.

*Rape Crisis Program*, New Bedford's Women's Center, 252 County St., New Bedford 02740. (617) 996-6656.

## MICHIGAN

*New Center Community Mental Health Services*, 2990 W. Grand Blvd., Suite 300, Detroit 48202. (313) 934-5200.

*Everywoman's Place—Crisis Center*, 1433 Clinton St., Muskegon 49442.

## MINNESOTA

*Programs for Victims of Sexual Assault*, 424 W. Superior St., 202 Ordeen Building, Duluth 55802. (218) 720-8344 (Toll-free in Minnesota).

*Sexual Violence Center of Hennepin County*, 1222 W. 31st St., Minneapolis 55408. (612) 824-5555.

## MISSISSIPPI

*Jackson Rape Crisis Center*, 748 N. President St., Jackson 39225. (601) 982-RAPE.

*Gulf Coast Women's Center*, P.O. Box 333, Biloxi 39533. (601) 436-3809.

## MISSOURI

*M.O.C.S.A.*, 106 E. 31st Terrace, Kansas City 64111. (816) 531-0233.

*Rape Crisis Assistance, Inc.*, 440 S. Market, Springfield 65806. (417) 866-6665.

## MONTANA

*Billings Rape Task Force*, 1245 N. 29th, Billings 59101. (406) 259-6506.

*Violence Free Crisis Line*, 723 5th Ave. E., Room 420, Kalispell 59901. (406) 752-7273.

*Women's Place*, 521 N. Orange St., Missoula 59802. (406) 543-7606.

## NEBRASKA

*Rape/Spouse Abuse Crisis Center*, 1133 "H" St., Lincoln 68508. (402) 471-7273.

## NEVADA

*Community Action Against Rape*, 749 Veterans Memorial Dr., Room 30, Las Vegas 89101. (702) 385-2153.

## NEW HAMPSHIRE

*Rape and Assault Support Services*, P.O. Box 217, Nashua 03061. (603) 883-3044.

*YWCA/Women's Crisis Service*, 72 Concord St., Manchester 03101. (603) 668-2922.

## NEW JERSEY

*Sexual Abuse and Assault Program*, St. Francis Counseling Service, 47th and Long Beach Blvd., Brant Beach 08008. (609) 494-1090 and (201) 370-4010.

*Sexual Assault and Rape Analysis Unit (SARA)*, 1 Lincoln Ave., Room 203, Newark 07104. (201) 733-7273.

## NEW MEXICO

*Helpline Rape Crisis Team*, 1408 8th St., Alamogordo 88310. (505) 437-8680.

*Albuquerque Rape Center*, 1025 Hermosa S.E., Albuquerque 87108. (505) 266-7711.

## NEW YORK

*Albany County Rape Crisis Center*, Room 640, 112 State St., Albany 12207. (518) 445-7547.

*Bora-Crisis Center*, Harlem Hospital, 506 Lenox Ave., New York City 10037. (212) 577-7777.

*Rape Crisis Program*, St. Vincent's Hospital and Medical Center, 153 W. 11th St., New York City 10011. (212) 790-7000 (ask for Rape Crisis Program).

*Rape Crisis Service of Planned Parenthood of Rochester and the Genesee Valley*, 114 University Ave., Rochester 14605. (716) 546-2777 (for Monroe County), 1-800-527-1757 (for surrounding areas).

*Victim Services Agency*, Bayley Seton Hospital, Bay St. and Vanderbilt Ave., Staten Island 10304. (718) 447-5454.

*Rape Crisis Services*, YWCA, 1000 Cornelia St., Utica 13502. (315) 733-0665.

## NORTH CAROLINA
*Durham YWCA Rape Crisis Center*, 809 Proctor Ave., Durham 27707. (919) 638-8628.
*Real Crisis Intervention, Inc.*, 312 E. 10th St., Greenville 27858. (919) 758-HELP.

## NORTH DAKOTA
*Grand Forks Abuse and Rape Crisis Center*, 111 S. 4th St., Grand Forks 58201. (701) 746-8900.
*Rape and Abuse Crisis Center*, P.O. Box 2984, Fargo 58108. (701) 293-7273.

## OHIO
*Women Helping Women, Inc.*, 216 E. 9th St., Cincinnati 54202. (513) 381-5616.
*National Assault Prevention Center*, P.O. Box 02005, Columbus 43202. (614) 291-2540.
*Women Against Rape*, P.O. Box 02084, Columbus 43202. (614) 221-4447.
*Cleveland Rape Crisis Center*, 3201 Euclid Ave., Cleveland 44118. (513) 747-2696.

## OKLAHOMA
*Women's Resource Center*, P.O. Box 5089, Norman 73069. (405) 360-0590.
*YWCA Rape Crisis Intervention Services*, 129 N.W. 5th St., Oklahoma City 73102.

## OREGON
*Center Against Rape and Domestic Violence*, P.O. Box 914, Corvallis 97339. (503) 754-0110.
*Jackson County Rape Crisis Council*, P.O. Box 819, Medford 97501. (503) 779-HELP.
*Victim Assistance Project*, 804 County Courthouse, Portland 97204. (503) 248-3222.
*Mid Valley Women's Crisis Service*, 990 Broadway N.E., Salem 97301. (503) 399-7722.

## PENNSYLVANIA

*Women Organized Against Rape*, 124 S. 9th St., Suite 601, Philadelphia 19107. (215) 922-3434.

*Pittsburgh Action Against Rape*, 3712 Forbes Ave., Pittsburgh 15213. (412) 765-2731.

## RHODE ISLAND

*Rhode Island Rape Crisis Center*, 1660 Broad St., Cranston 02905. (401) 941-2400.

*Newport County Community Mental Health, Inc.*, 65 Valley Rd., Middletown 02840. (401) 846-1213.

## SOUTH CAROLINA

*People Against Rape*, 701 E. Bay St., BTC Box 1101, Charleston 29403. (803) 722-7273.

*Rape Crisis of Greenville*, 700 Augusta St., Greenville 29605. (803) 233-4357.

*Tri-County CASA*, P.O. Box 1568, Orangeburg 29116. (803) 534-2272.

## SOUTH DAKOTA

*Aberdeen Area Rape Task Force*, P.O. Box 41, Aberdeen 57402. (605) 226-1212.

*Rape Education, Advocacy, and Counseling Team (REACT)*, 802 11th Ave., Brookings 57006. (605) 692-7233.

## TENNESSEE

*Women's Resource and Rape Assistance Program*, 416 E. Lafayette, Jackson 38301. (901) 423-0700.

*The Rape and Sexual Abuse Center*, P.O. Box 120831, Nashville 37217. (615) 327-1110.

## TEXAS

*Rape Crisis/Domestic Violence Center*, 804 S. Bryan, Suite 214, Amarillo 79106. (806) 373-8022.

*Rape Crisis and Child Sexual Abuse Center*, 899 Stemmons Freeway, Suite 1186, Dallas 57235. (214) 653-8740.

## UTAH

*YWCA/Women's Crisis Center*, 505 27th St., Ogden 84403. (801) 392-7273.

*Victim Service Agency*, 231 E. 400 S., Salt Lake City 84111. (801) 363-7900.

## VERMONT

*Women's Crisis Center*, P.O. Box 933, Brattleboro 05301. (802) 254-6954.

*Women's Rape Crisis Center*, P.O. Box 92, Burlington 05402. (802) 863-1236.

## VIRGINIA

*Rape Victim Companion Program*, Office on Women, 2525 Mt. Vernon Ave., Unit 6, Alexandria 22301. (703) 683-7273.

*Bristol Crisis Center*, P.O. Box 642, Bristol 24201. (703) 466-2312.

*Women's Resource Center of the New River Valley*, P.O. Box 306, Radford 24141. (703) 639-1123.

*YWCA Women's Advocacy Program*, 6 N. 5th St., Richmond 23219. (804) 643-0888.

## WASHINGTON D.C. (See District of Columbia)

## WASHINGTON (Alphabetical by city)

*Grays Harbor Rape Crisis Services*, P.O. Box 423, Aberdeen 98520. (206) 532-8639.

*North Kitsap Advocates for Sexually Assaulted People*, P.O. Box 11678, Bainbridge Island 98110.

*Whatcom County Crisis Services*, 124 E. Holly, Room 201, Bellingham 98225. (206) 734-7271.

*Kitsap Sexual Assault Center*, P.O. Box 1327, Bremerton 98310. (206) 479-8500.

*Care Services*, P.O. Box 337, Chehalis 98532. (206) 748-6601 or 1-800-458-3080.

*Alternatives to Violence*, 605 S. Infirmary Road, Colville 99114. (509) 684-6139.

*Domestic Violence/Rape Relief*, 220 W. 4th, Ellensburg 98926. (509) 925-4168.

**WASHINGTON** (continued)

*Providence Sexual Assault Center*, P.O. Box 1067, Everett 98206. (206) 252-4800.

*Forks Abuse Program*, P.O. Box 1775, Forks 98331. (206) 374-2273.

*Sexual Assault Program*, Madigan Army Medical Center, P.O. Box 52, Ft. Lewis 98431.

*Volunteers Against Violence*, P.O. Box 325, Friday Harbor 98250. (206) 562-6025.

*Skagit Rape Relief/Battered Women's Services*, P.O. Box 301, Mt. Vernon 98273. (206) 336-9591.

*Pacific County Crisis Support Network*, P.O. Box 189, Naselle 98638. 1-800-HELP-CSN.

*Family Crisis Support Network*, P.O. Box 959, Newport 99156. (509) 447-5483.

*Citizens Against Domestic Abuse*, P.O. Box 190, Oak Harbor 98277. (206) 675-2232.

*Safeplace*, P.O. Box 1605, Olympia 98507. (206) 754-6300.

*The Support Center*, P.O. Box 2058, Omak 98841. (509) 826-3221.

*Safehome/Rape Relief*, 101 E. Midway Business Center #21, Port Angeles 98362. (206) 452-HELP.

*Domestic Violence/Sexual Assault Program*, P.O. Box 743, Port Townsend 98368. (206) 385-5291.

*King County Rape Relief*, 1025 S. 3rd, Suite C, Renton 98057. (206) 226-7273.

*Ferry County Community Services*, P.O. Box 406, Republic 99166. (509) 775-3341.

*The Sexual Assault Response Center*, 640 Jadwin Ave., Suite D, Richland 99352. (509) 946-2377 (24-hour).

*Center for the Prevention of Sexual and Domestic Violence*, 1914 N. 34th St., Suite 105, Seattle 98103. (206) 634-1903 (Referrals only).

*Seattle Rape Relief*, 1825 S. Jackson, Seattle 98144. (206) 632-7273.

*Sexual Assault Center*, Harborview Medical Center, 1401 E. Jefferson, Seattle 98104. (206) 223-3047.

*Recovery*, P.O. Box 1132, Shelton 98584. (206) 426-5878.

*Rape Crisis Network*, S. 7 Howard, Suite 200, Spokane 99204. (509) 747-8224.

**WASHINGTON** (continued)

*Skamania County Council on Domestic Violence and Sexual Assault*, P.O. Box 477, Stevenson 98648. (509) 427-5636.

*Family Violence and Sexual Assault Center*, P.O. Box 93, Sunnyside 98944. (509) 837-6689.

*Pierce County Rape Relief*, S. 19th and Union, Tacoma 98405. (206) 474-RAPE.

*Clark County Sexual Assault Program*, 1115 Esther St., Vancouver 98660. (206) 695-0501.

*Community Abuse and Assault Center Helpline*, P.O. Box 1773, Walla Walla 99363. (509) 529-3377.

*Wenatchee Rape Crisis Center*, P.O. Box 2704, Wenatchee 98801. (509) 663-7446.

*Sexual Assault Unit*, 321 E. Yakima Ave., Yakima 98907. (509) 575-4200.

**WEST VIRGINIA**

*Sexual Assault Services of Family Services of Kanawha Valley*, 922 Quarrier St., #201, Charleston 25301. (304) 340-3676.

*Hancock-Brooke Mental Health Service*, 501 Colliers Way, Weirton 26062. (304) 797-5000.

**WISCONSIN**

*New Horizons for Domestic Violence*, YWCA, P.O. Box 2031, LaCrosse 54601. (608) 784-6419.

*Dane County Rape Crisis Center*, 147 S. Butler, Madison 53703. (608) 251-7273.

**WYOMING**

*Sweetwater County Task Force on Sexual Assault*, 450 S. Main, Rock Springs 82901. (307) 382-4381.

Carolyn M. Byerly, author
*Photo: C. Mendoza*

# About the Author

Carolyn M. Byerly, Ph.D., teaches journalism and international communications at Radford University in southwestern Virginia. Dr. Byerly's professional background is in journalism, public relations, and nonprofit agency administration.

Her involvement with the problems of sexual and domestic violence date to the late 1970s, when she began volunteering as a rape crisis counselor at a community rape relief program. In 1979 she assumed the administrative coordination for Thurston County Rape Relief, and a year later for the newly established Safeplace women's shelter and rape crisis center, Olympia, Washington.

While in this position (1979-84), she also chaired an interagency group, the Thurston County Committee on Child Abuse and Neglect; helped design child sexual abuse prevention programs for public schools; and participated in educational events aimed at expanding public awareness of sexual and domestic violence. She held offices in the Washington Coalition of Sexual Assault Programs, 1979-82, and the National Coalition Against Sexual Assault, 1984-87.

Dr. Byerly continues to work with community agencies and the survivors of violence to improve public information about these problems.

# ORDER FORM
for additional copies of
## *THE MOTHER'S BOOK*

Name_____

Organization_____

Address_____
           (Street)

_____
      (City)               (State)        (Zip)

Phone   Home ( )_____
           Area Code      (Number)
       Work ( )_____
           Area Code      (Number)

Number of Copies_____ @ $6.95 per copy    $_____

Shipping/Handling Costs:  1 copy —    $2.00
                    2-10 copies —  $4.00    $_____

Washington Residents add 8.2% Sales Tax    $_____

                    TOTAL Enclosed  $_____

ALL ORDERS MUST BE PREPAID

Make check payable to CPSDV and mail with this completed form to:

**CENTER FOR THE PREVENTION OF
SEXUAL AND DOMESTIC VIOLENCE (CPSDV)**
1914 N. 34th Street, Suite 105
Seattle, Washington 98103
(206) 634-1903
FAX (206) 634-0115

BULK ORDERS:
For orders of 11 or more, please place your order through Kendall/Hunt Publishing Company at (800) 338-5578.  Bulk discounts available.

*The Center for the Prevention of Sexual and Domestic Violence is a private, nonprofit, interreligious educational organization whose mission is to end sexual and domestic violence by working through churches, synagogues, and seminaries in the United States and Canada.*